19-73

Category Formation and the History of Religions

Religion and Reason 1

Method and Theory
in the Study and Interpretation of Religion

MOUTON · THE HAGUE · PARIS

Category Formation
and
the History of Religions

by

ROBERT D. BAIRD

School of Religion
University of Iowa

MOUTON · THE HAGUE · PARIS

Library of Congress Catalog Card Number: 76-152081

Preface

It is necessary to indicate the relationship between the method here articulated and another work on 'Indian Religious Traditions' which I have contributed to a book on man's religions. While I think I avoided certain methodological mistakes in that work, it was completed before the present method was entirely worked out. In that essay I did not always ask the 'religiohistorical' question of the data, although I was beginning to move in that direction. Hence that essay on religion in India is only a dim illustration of the present method. Such a concession does not mean that the method is inapplicable. Its application is the goal of my present researches.

In any work of this nature, there are intellectual debts which can never be repaid. Even those thinkers with whom one disagrees most sharply are responsible for clarifying issues in the mind of the one who rejects their positions. Although it may not always be apparent, I am particularly indebted to the work of Wilfred Cantwell Smith. While I have not always accepted Professor Smith's answers, his questions have opened new areas for methodological discussion. My differences with him should not completely conceal this debt.

A note of appreciation is due to my students at the University of Iowa, whose searching questions have helped to sharpen the approach here set forth. This approach has been enriched by my encounter with students, and will hopefully continue to inform and enrich my teaching.

Mr. Raymond Rohrbaugh and Mr. George M. Williams, graduate students in religion, have read the manuscript and have made valuable suggestions regarding style and content. My colleague, Professor Robert P. Scharlemann, has read the manuscript thoroughly and has given freely of his time in a discussion which is probably not over yet. Of course, none of the above are responsible for any error of fact or judgment which might remain.

Finally, as any scholar knows, a supportive family is an inestimable asset. To my family this volume is dedicated.

Robert D. Baird

Acknowledgments

The author wishes to thank the following journals for permission to use his own material previously published in article form:

The Journal of Religious Thought, for 'Syncretism and the History of Religions', Vol. XXIV, No. 2, 1967–68, pp. 42–53. Also for 'Factual Statements and the Possibility of Objectivity in History', Vol. XXVI, No. 1, 1969, pp. 5–22.

History and Theory, for 'Interpretative Categories and the History of Religions', Beiheft 8, 1968, pp. 17–30.

Union Seminary Quarterly Review, for 'Normative Elements in Eliade's Phenomenology of Symbolism', Vol. XXV, No. 4, pp. 505–516.

The author is also indebted to the following for permission to reprint copyrighted material:

Sheed and Ward, for *Patterns in Comparative Religion* by Mircea Eliade.

Hans Küng, for 'The World Religions in God's Plan of Salvation', in *Christian Revelation and World Religions*.

Wilfred Cantwell Smith for *The Faith of Other Men*.

The New American Library, Inc., for *The Meaning and End of Religion* by Wilfred Cantwell Smith.

Charles Scribner's Sons, for *Questions of Religious Truth* by Wilfred Cantwell Smith.

Clarendon Press, Oxford, for *Definition* by Richard Robinson.

The University of Chicago Press, for *History of Religions: Essays in Methodology*, edited by Mircea Eliade and Joseph M. Kitagawa.

Lutterworth Press, for *Religion and the Christian Faith* by Hendrik Kraemer.

Harper and Row Publishers, for *Myth and Reality* and *Rites and Symbols of Initiation: The Mysteries of Birth and Rebirth*, both by Mircea Eliade.

Contents

Contents

The Nature of Category Formation

The history of religions has not been prone to engage in academic isolationism. Its willingness to accept and even be dominated by other disciplines has been part of its history. From early evolutionary theories of religious development and anthropological discussions about animism and the origin of religion up to more recent historical and phenomenological methods, historians of religions have exhibited their willingness to learn from scholars in other disciplines. Phenomenological methods invaded *Religionswissenschaft* rather late in comparison with other fields.[1] The same has been said for the comparative method.[2] The dependence of history of religions on other disciplines is hardly more clear than in Mircea Eliade's article 'The History of Religions in Retrospect: 1912 and After'.[3] The majority of scholars surveyed would not be considered historians of religions in any strict sense. If anthropologists, sociologists, depth psychologists, and social anthropologists are also to be called historians of religions, then the latter badge becomes even more ambiguous than it already is. Furthermore, most of the above do not consider themselves historians of religions and would have as much difficulty in defining the discipline of history of religions as the historian of religions seems to be having.

It is because historians of religions have been so receptive to methods from other disciplines that the total lack of influence in the area of definitional procedures is so curious. Anthropologists, sociologists, physical scientists, and logicians have, with considerable insight and rigor, shed light on the nature of language and definition. More often than not historians of religions have ignored definitional problems. When they do discuss the matter they show an almost complete lack of philosophic sophistication regarding the meaning or significance of a definition. Historians of religions tend to assume that a definition is a definition, and that it is as clear as the word 'religion'. Neither term ('religion' or 'definition') needs to be clarified since we know what both of them mean. Both assumptions are false.

'Definition' is itself an ambiguous word.[4] Definitions have been classified and analyzed in various ways by logicians.[5] While an analysis of category formation is not a cure for all our problems, it could point us in the right direction, or at least enable us to determine if we are operating appropriately. Our goal will be not to exhaust the topic of definition, but to utilize some logical distinctions because of their usefulness for history of religions methodology. But first we must turn to an analysis of what might be called a dominant motif in the history of religions today. The dominance of this motif is all the more critical since it is found among both those whom Eliade calls 'phenomenologists' and those whom he calls 'historicists'.[6]

A. ESSENTIAL-INTUITIONAL METHOD

By intuitional I mean a method in which the historian of religions does not recognize a need to begin his work with a definition of 'religion', thereby marking the limits and extent of his study. This method assumes that we all know what is meant by the word, and that, given room for accidental differences, 'religion' is essentially unambiguous. This introduces the other aspect of this method: essentialism or realism. It means (by implication and method) that religion is a something out there whose 'essence' can be apprehended by the historian of religions.[7]

A frequent companion of this notion is the assumption that there is some natural connection between the word and the reality to which it refers. Without this assumption, it would make little sense to assume that the mere announcement of the word 'religion' would erase all ambiguity and enable us to proceed toward our goal, whatever it may be. The essential-intuitional method, then, proceeds as though the word 'religion' corresponds to something that has univocal ontological status, that the word is unambiguous, and that the reality or essence which it names is intuitively identifiable.

The essential-intuitional method is widely used, often without explicitly raising such basic questions. Occasionally it becomes *somewhat* more explicit.[8] If the question of definitions arises at all (and frequently it does not), it arises at the *end* of one's study, or perhaps even at the end of one's career.[9] The significance of this will become abundantly clear.

In the two-volume work by George Foot Moore,[10] one finds no discussion of methodology. Moore was an historian intent on applying his historical method to the study of religion. He approached his material intending to deal with 'religious conceptions, as they are implicit in myth and ritual or are thought out by poets, philosophers, and prophets; and particularly to the higher developments in theology, ethics, and religious philosophy...'.[11] His effort would also include relating religion to race, physical environment, and civilization. Nowhere did Moore find it necessary to venture a definition of religion as a prior methodological necessity for his work. The assumption is that when we talk about 'religion' or 'religions', we all know what that means. There are the religions of India, China and Japan (Hinduism, Buddhism, and Taoism, to name a few), and Egypt, Babylonia, Greece, and Rome. Then there are Christianity, Judaism, and Islam. That these words might be ambiguous does not enter into Moore's deliberations.

Moore is quite able to see a unity amidst the religious diversity, a unity which takes the form of an evolutionary trend. Each one of these intuitively identified religions, however, must be studied in its historical completeness in order to be understood. Moore held that historians of religions have mistakenly devoted themselves to origins without taking account of the many changes and variations through which the religions have gone. George Foot Moore's procedure betrays the essential-intuitional method.

Mircea Eliade also proceeds intuitively. In the foreword of his book *Patterns in Comparative Religion*, he affirms his desire to study the religious phenomena as something religious.[12] He makes a correlation between religion and 'the element of the sacred'. While explicitly stating that one of the problems his volume is attempting to answer is 'what is religion'?[13] he nevertheless doubts the value of beginning with a definition of the religious phenomena.

> As I doubt the value of beginning with a definition of the religious phenomenon, I am simply going to examine various 'hierophanies' – taking that term in its widest sense as anything that manifests the sacred.[14]

Rather than define 'the sacred', Eliade reiterates, by quoting Roger Callois, that it is difficult to define. The assumption is, of course, that it is nevertheless readily identifiable. However complex the labyrinth of facts might be, they are identifiable – even though they cannot be reduced to a handy definition.

> At bottom, the only helpful thing that one can say of the sacred in general is contained in the very definition of the term: that it is the opposite of the

profane. As soon as one attempts to give a clear definition of the nature, the *modality* of that opposition, one strikes difficulty. No formula, however elementary, will cover the labyrinthine complexity of the facts.[15] That Eliade proceeds intuitively is beyond dispute when we read: 'We are dispensed from any *a priori* definition of the religious phenomenon; the reader can make his own reflections on the nature of the sacred as he goes'.[16]

It is this essential-intuitional approach which is usually used in determining the validity or invalidity of certain definitions of religion. C. J. Bleeker argues against short phrase definitions of religion by stating that '. . . religion is a far too complex entity to be covered by a short phrase'.[17] He further points out that the key term of power as utilized by Van der Leeuw is too broad. '. . . Besides divine power there is also demonical and satanical power'.[18] Others tried to guarantee 'against the danger that the definition of religion would include non-religious phenomena'[19] by stressing man's relationship to a higher personal power. But in so defining religion, Bleeker feels that K. L. Bellon goes too far.

> In consequence of his principles Bellon cuts out big and essential parts of the history of religions, i.e. a great deal of primitive religion and of the religions of India and China, mysticism, pantheism and even Buddhism, a powerful world religion.[20]

To so define the term is to cut out phenomena 'of which the religious quality can hardly be doubted'.[21] Rudolf Otto's 'numinous' tended to ignore the obvious point that 'Religion is an affair of the community'.[22] When Bleeker himself moves toward 'the divine' as the key to religion on the basis that '. . . it can be stated without contradiction that theoretically religion always has been and still is man's relation to a superhuman power',[23] one can almost hear other essential-intuitionalists calling from the wings that such a definition cuts us off from the Pāli tradition of the Buddha's teaching which theoretically eliminates superhuman power as relevant to man's quest for the extinction of suffering.

While there are significant differences between Mircea Eliade and C. J. Bleeker, they are united in proceeding with the essential-intuitional method. They are finally after the 'essence' of religion, and both feel that such must be the conclusion of the study and not the starting point. While Eliade seldom lets on that he is aware of what he is doing, Bleeker is more explicit and indeed confesses the intuitive dimension with which we have been dealing.

The student of the history of religions and of the phenomenology of religion starts his study with an *intuitive*, hardly formulated, axiomatic notion of what religion is. His ultimate aim is an inclusive formulation of the essence of religion.[24]

A. Eustace Haydon, in surveying progress in the history of religions during the first quarter of the twentieth century, indicates that some clarification of the nature of religion has taken place '*partly because of a better knowledge of religions*, partly because of the new scientific approach'.[25] Haydon indicates that the *a priori* is never so subtle as it is in the study of religion. He points out that when religion was defined as belief in spiritual or supernatural beings, it was then necessary to say that 'Confucianism' and other systems where gods do not figure to any significant extent are not religious. They are mere ethical systems. It might be pointed out that one still hears the rather outdated and naive question asked as to whether 'Buddhism' or 'Confucianism' or sometimes 'Taoism' is a religion. Haydon held that the result of further study of religions had led to more accurate definitions such as 'faith in the conservation of values' or the 'shared quest for a completely satisfying life'. However, in spite of the attempt to avoid all appearance of the *a priori*, the essential-intuitional position appears again. The growing definitional clarity, if one can call it that, is the result of greater acquaintance with the religions, and not by reason of any greater analytical clarity.

In a more recent survey of the history of religions, Philip Ashby finds it unnecessary to say anything about progress made with the definitional problem. Whether that is because he deems it unimportant, or because no significant progress has been made is another question. He does indicate that the history of religions is 'an area of scholarly pursuit in search for a definition of itself'.[26] I would suggest that it is unlikely that we will come to know what the history of religions means or ought to mean until we know what is meant by one of the basic terms involved: 'religion'. As a step in that direction, we now turn to a discussion of types of definition.

B. TYPES OF DEFINITION

That historians of religions have tended to proceed with the study of religions without an explicit definition seems to have been an attempt to avoid an unwarranted *a priori*. This would distinguish them from both theologians and philosophers of religion. Basically this was a desire to address some questions in the study of religion that could not be answered theologically, but only by an appeal to historical data. However, little actual progress has been made in asking the religious question by failure to distinguish between questions that can be answered only by an examination of data, and questions for which a study of data will never yield answers. We have labored hard under a basic misunderstanding of the nature and use of religio-historical categories which can not be settled merely by familiarity with an abundance of data.

Anthropologists have had to be reminded of this basic distinction. There is a certain analogy between their attempt at a definition of 'culture' and our attempt at a definition of 'religion'. In this context Leslie A. White makes an inescapable observation equally applicable to the search of historians of religions for a definition of religion.

> Until anthropologists distinguish clearly between two quite different kinds of problems... in short, until they distinguish sharply between *things and events* in the external world, and *verbal concepts* with which these phenomena are represented, they will continue to grope and flounder, trying to discover what culture 'basically is', striving for 'greater precision of definition'.[27]

Logicians have classified these as kinds of definitions. The most common division is between nominal and real definitions, the former referring to the meaning assigned to *nomina* or words, the latter referring to the 'essence' of *res* or things. Nominal definitions have also been subdivided, and if Richard Robinson's analysis is correct, the search for real definitions does not proceed in only one direction either.[28] I would like to deal with three types of 'definitions' at this point because they illuminate certain methodological problems faced by the historian of religions. First I will offer a brief definition of each type after which I will deal with them in somewhat more detail.

1. A *functional definition* is the act of stipulating that a certain word means a certain thing (a thing meaning any objective reality including other words, the meanings of which are already known).

2. A *lexical definition* 'is that sort of word-thing definition in which we are explaining the actual way in which some actual word has been used by some actual person'.[29]

3. A *real definition* is a true statement about things that are.

A *functional definition* is semi-arbitrary. Usually it is stated that stipulative definitions are purely arbitrary. I have chosen the word functional instead of stipulative in order to indicate that the historian of religions is not interested in purely formal analysis, but is after definitions that are usable. Hence they are semi-arbitrary. This does not mean that they are determined by an examination of data or that their legitimacy is to be tested by available data. The functional definition is arbitrary in that there is no inherent reason why any word cannot be used for any thing. Logically one could define 'religion' as equivalent to the three angles of a triangle, but that would not get us very far. Hence, while functional definitions are in principle free or arbitrary and are not derived as a result of an examination of data, they are not formulated in ignorance of the data. Only if one is familiar with the data will he have any insight into meaningful questions that might be asked of them. Hence functional definitions are semi-arbitrary in that they are *not proved* by data-documentation, but are thereby judged as to their *applicability* and *usefulness*.

A further implication of the functional definition derives from its nominal character.

> In contrast to all... varieties of truth-asserting definitions, a 'nominal' definition is a suggestion to name a phenomenon in a given way without implying anything about the scientific propositions relating to this phenomenon. Thus, nominal definitions are devoid of hypotheses. They cannot be true or false. They can be clumsy or elegant, appropriate or inappropriate, effective or worthless – but not true or false.[30]

Since the functional definition is nominal, it is not only semi-arbitrary, but also lacks truthvalue. It is a resolve to use a certain word in a certain way and hence one cannot ask if the definition is true, nor is it appropriate to test its truth by examining data. The question 'is it true' is only applicable to lexical and real definitions. Although in principle arbitrary, frequently a functional definition is equivalent to deciding which of several meanings of a word is to be adopted for the purposes at hand.

> Whether this individual choice agrees with or differs from the common usage of the word defined, and whether there *is* any common usage of it or not, is irrelevant to the essence of stipulation. A stipulative definition may vary, in this respect, all the way from stipulating an entirely novel noise as the name of an entirely novel thing, to merely confirming and adopting common usage. Often it consists merely in adopting one of the many common meanings of a common word and discarding the rest, that

is, in announcing which of the established meanings you are going to use.[31]

The arbitrary aspect of functional definitions is based on the belief that there is no natural or necessary connection between words or things. One point is reasonably sure: people do not acquire meanings for words that are never used around them.

...there is no connection between a word and the thing it means except that some human beings use that word to mean that thing. There is no connection between the word 'cock-a-doodle-doo' and the cry of a cock except that some people use the one sound to mean the other sound, and mistakenly think that the two sounds resemble each other.[32]

Functional definitions lend precision to a study by removing ambiguity in words. That most words are ambiguous (having more than one meaning) should be clear by a glance at a large dictionary which, among other things, records lexical definitions for each word. A functional definition makes a word unambiguous by stipulating that for a given work it means a single thing. The precision of the functional definition is dependent on the clarity of our language and not on the data. Hence one cannot say a certain functional definition of 'religion' or 'magic' lacks precision because of what it includes or excludes, though one might judge it because it is not useful.

As for 'precision of definitions', definitions are not more or less precise – like measurements of the velocity of light. A definition of *bug* that includes spiders is neither more nor less precise than one that does not. Needless to say, a 'definition' that does not mark boundaries, set limits, in shorts, which does not define, is not a definition...To be sure, a definition may be precise without being useful or fruitful in scientific interpretation.[33]

Somewhat related to the question of precision is a cluster of objections to such definitional procedures on the grounds that some terms (such as 'religion') are indefinable, or that religious experience is ineffable. Let us first address ourselves to the question of indefinability. This seems to refer to words, while the proposal of ineffability seems to refer to things. There is a basic reason which encourages people to hold that some words are indefinable, and that is the unrecognized ambiguity of these words. If, not recognizing that a word has more than one meaning, we seek its 'univocal sense', upon finding that each proposed meaning fails to cover one of the current meanings, we will conclude that the term is indefinable.[34] Any word is capable of functional or lexical definition. We are not recommending language games which *require* that *all* words be *explicitly* defined under the cloak of a legitimate search for meaning. Many words communicate anyway and hence in a given setting may not require functional or lexical definition.[35]

Robinson's remark about lexical definitions would be equally valid for functional ones, for if all communicable signs have had a meaning, they can also continue to do so.

> Our doctrine is that every communicable sign is lexically definable. For no sign can be used in communication unless its meaning can be made known to the person with whom you wish to communicate. If therefore any sign is lexically indefinable to Mr. A, that sign is useless for communicating with Mr. A; and if any sign is lexically indefinable to everybody, that sign is useless for all communication. In other words, all signs successfully used in communication are lexically definable.[36]

The argument of ineffability seems to be directed to things. It seems to say that there are some things which cannot be expressed or named. Here again there seems to be a basic reason why one should be led to such a position. Functional definitions depend on the availability of both the word and the thing. Words communicate, that is they have meaning only if two or more persons use the same word to express the same experience. This type of word meaning is possible whenever an experience or object is open to more than one person. But we are often led to attribute ineffability to an experience because the word we use to name it does not correspond to any thing experienced by another. But, 'nothing is ineffable in the sense of being unnameable by its experiencer'.[37]

> 'Ineffable' seems to mean unspeakable; but, whereas a thing may be unspeakable merely because it is too horrible or because there is a taboo against naming it, the ineffable is intended to be that sort of unspeakableness which no human, however emancipated, could possibly overcome because it is inherent in the nature of the thing in its relation to the nature of symbols... In this trivial sense, then, the unknown is ineffable so long as it remains unknown; and if anything is necessarily for ever unknowable, it is necessarily also for ever ineffable.
>
> But the ineffability that anyone is interested in asserting is the ineffability of something that can be known and is known. Is that possible?[38]

If, then, some experience is the possession of only a small minority of persons, they will be able to communicate it to each other but not to the majority. This is why such terms as *śūnyatā* or *satori* are difficult in purely academic work-they presuppose an experience which the majority of persons have not had.

One not infrequently encounters resistance to the very request for functional definitions on the grounds that it is a useless and time-consuming enterprise. The definition of words tends to make us preoccupied with words when we should be concerned with the nature of things. But as long as words continue to be a means to a knowledge of things, we must continue to sharpen this cutting edge of the discipline.

> Tools cannot be used well without being also contemplated from time to time. Their use must be learnt. In the case of words, learning to use them is a word-thing definition. And the study of word-thing definition corresponds to critical reflection on one's current methods of learning the use of tools, to see whether it can be improved.[39]

A *lexical definition*, since it asserts that a certain word has had a certain meaning to someone sometime, is, unlike the functional definition, either true or false. Lexical definitions, then, are true or false because they are historical statements. The resolve which someone made to use a certain word in a certain way is neither true nor false, but 'a statement that certain people observe a certain rule is either true or false, and a lexical definition is such a statement'.[40]

Morton Smith holds that the question of the nature of religion, i.e. the definition of the word, is a historical question and not a philosophical one.[41] He is disturbed when he finds philosophers inventing their own meaning for such terms and then going through history forcing religions into that mold. However, although he sees the definition of the term as basically an historical question, given the vast variety of usages he doubts if the question is answerable.

> Therefore I think the best we can do, with questions of this sort, is to content ourselves with the customary generalities produced by the superficial, historical methods of lexicography, and proceed to discuss the role of historical method in the study of religion without knowing exactly what we are talking about.[42]

Smith then goes on to indicate how the historical method is to be applied to the study of religion, presumably 'without knowing exactly what we are talking about'. It is difficult indeed to see what textual criticism or the historical background of texts can contribute to the study of something whose identity is unclear. One might almost be tempted to conclude that Smith is 'putting us on' and that he simply has an avid sense of humor were it not for the fact that this is what we as historians of religions have been generally prone to do- make studies of 'religion' without knowing exactly what we are talking about.

But Morton Smith oversimplifies the definitional problem. History cannot give us more than lexical definitions, that is, evidence that the term has been used in such and such a way at such a time by such a person or group. Lexical definitions do not eliminate ambiguity. Only functional definitions can do that. That such a procedure could ever produce a real definition or the 'essence' of the thing presupposes that there is no existing ambiguity in the term. We will shortly show that this is not the case. Indeed, there need be no connection between how the term has been used and how it ought to be used, although one would not deliberately seek to avoid all past usages.

A *real definition* points to acquiring knowledge about things. Such 'definitions' are not only true or false, but presumably come at the end of a study. One also expects some form of proof. It is inconceivable that a functional definition should come at the end of a book since it determines how an otherwise ambiguous word will be used. But a discussion of the nature of the thing to which a word unambiguously refers could only come after an analysis of that thing.

When Socrates and Plato discussed definition, they had 'real definition' in mind and not functional definitions.[43] This involved the search for the 'essence' of the thing. Robinson suggests that the search for an essence is misdirected since there does not appear to be any such thing.[44]

> Essence, then, is just the human choice of what to mean by a name, misinterpreted as being a metaphysical reality. The essence of x is the proposition that 'the word x is defined to mean yz', misunderstood as the proposition that 'x is yz', where the expression 'x' and 'yz' are thought to have different meanings, although in reality they have the same meaning because the expression 'x' is defined as meaning yz.[45]

At least it must be said that the meaning of 'essence' is unclear and must be defined if it is to be a legitimate goal for the historian of religions.

The search for an 'essence' is frequently an attempt to find an identity in the numerous applications of an ambiguous word. There is no point to asking 'But what really is x?' when it has been shown that 'x' is ambiguous.

> And every man who seeks a real definition of the thing x ought to ask
> himself first whether he has good reason to believe that he is not referring
> to more than one thing by his word 'x'. Until we have isolated and chosen
> a single sense of the word 'x', it is necessarily misleading to start asking
> for a real definition of the thing x.[46]

The 'real definition'[47] of a thing is nothing more than an analysis of that thing
and therefore involves statements about it which can be verified with various
forms of data. But such 'real definitions' or truth-assertions, fail unless the
words therein have been rendered unambiguous by functional definitions.

The search for an 'essence' often takes another subtle form: the recommendation of an ideal. Edward J. Jurji emphasizes that the phenomena of religion
are existential and transcendent.[48] Furthermore it is not reducible to its
function in society. He seems to define religion as did Rudolf Otto when he
says that 'Religious essence is technically known as the numinous'.[49] This,
however, is not a functional definition, but a type of 'real definition'. He is not
content to define the use of the term so as to mark out the limits of his study.
He is intending to define a thing, a reality. But Jurji goes even further than that.
Hidden in this definition is the actual endeavor to offer a proposal for allegiance.
Robinson indicates that this is one form of the search for a 'real definition'.

> The search for real definitions is sometimes, eighthly a search for ideals,
> an endeavor to choose what things to value and what flag to follow; and
> the announcement of real definitions is sometimes the announcement of
> one's allegiance and the act of persuading others to adopt the same
> ideals.[50]

This could not be more clear than when Jurji states:

> Real religion is not just an expression of society, a symptom of sickness
> in the soul. Religion is hardly ever at its best as adjunct to national stature,
> worldly power, or glory of culture.[51]

But Jurji uses within this volume, and even within a single sentence, two
meanings of the ambiguous word 'religious' without clearly distinguishing
them. He also identifies religions with the various categories of 'Hinduism,'
'Buddhism', etc. Hence one meets the statement that 'this numinous is in all
religions'.[52] This is not a functional definition. That it is, under the guise of the
search for an 'essence', the recommendation of a point of view, is seen in the
motivation for the proposal.

To find the essence of religion beneath various religions is to further

mutual understanding and appreciation. What is even more important, it is to further knowledge of the truth.[53]
Hence scientism, humanism, nationalism, secularism, historicism, and communism are modern *rivals* of *religious* faith, according to Jurji. If one were to offer the numinous as a functional definition this would be legitimate for it would be stipulating one among several meanings for an otherwise ambiguous word. But that Jurji is offering a 'real definition', an 'essence', is explicit. This functions as a means of encouraging the reader to adopt a certain view without philosophical argumentation.

We have argued that a search for the 'essence' of 'religion' is misdirected. We have also suggested that the search for an 'essence' is often a search for an identity of meaning in an ambiguous word. 'Religion' is such a word. One could write an entire volume in support of this, but it is hardly necessary. The point is adequately proved by choosing two definitions of religion which are current to show that they include and exclude different things which are commonly accepted as 'religious' when the word is intuitively (and ambiguously) applied.

C. J. Bleeker's statement that 'religion always has been and still is man's relation to a superhuman power'[54] eliminates not only Marxism but also the Pāli tradition and 'Confucianism' as well. Under Paul Tillich's definition that religion is 'ultimate concern'[55] not only are the Pāli tradition and 'Confucianism' forms of religion, but so are Marxism and secularism. It is irrelevant to ask which definition is true or even more true than the other – our point is that functional definitions are neither true nor false. But this does show that two explicit definitions of 'religion' are quite different. It is not helpful to suggest that they only *appear* different but are essentially the same if we could only see it. Such an argument must accept the correlative judgment that if they ever do *appear* to be identical, in essence they *really* are not if we could only see it.

Such ambiguity of general word usage is common. The word 'fast' is a good illustration since it is a word in which we lack the investment which we think we have in the word 'religion'. We say a horse is 'fast' if it can win a race, but also 'fast' when securely tied. We also say colors are 'fast' if they do not fade into each other when a garment is washed. Not to eat is to 'fast', and some undergraduates have a reputation for being 'fast' by reason of the way they conduct themselves on a date. Now what could it possibly mean to ask what is the 'real' meaning of the word 'fast'? What could its 'essence' possibly be?

Now the diverse meanings that have been given to 'religion' are equally varied. The reason why we have been unable to find a 'real definition' for the, term 'religion' is that the word has not referred to any one thing. Hence any definition that is offered as a 'real definition' for all that has commonly been included under the term 'religion' is found to be lacking because it either includes too much or too little *in terms of universal usage*. Now if this is true, then the history of religions is not only unable to begin with the 'given religions', assuming that we all know what that means, but if it has as its goal a final 'real definition' of the 'essence' of all religion, it is doomed to failure. It is doomed to failure not because we are not bright enough or do not live long enough to accumulate sufficient data to do the job, but because however much data we accumulate, it will not reveal an 'essence' since the word is ambiguous in general usage and therefore refers to more than one thing. It is a recognition of the ambiguity of the word 'religion' that led Wilfred Cantwell Smith to suggest that we discard the term altogether. He has subjected it to historical study in terms of its usage in the Western world and has found not one but at least four rather distinct meanings for the term.[56] Professor Smith was correct in concluding that no historical study of the term could give us a definition that would apply to all usages. This is not the nature of lexical definitions. But he was wrong in dropping the term on that account. For, as I have argued elsewhere,[57] the term 'faith' which he offers in its place, is equally ambiguous. And, what can be done to save a precise and unreified meaning for 'faith', i.e. offer a functional definition, can also be done for 'religion'.

C. FUNCTIONAL-DEFINITIONAL METHOD

By definitional we mean a method in which the historian of religions recognizes the need for the definition of categories at the beginning of his work. One recognizes the ambiguity of 'religion' and offers a functional definition in order that the word can have a single meaning. This also sets the limits of applicability of the method.

It is not merely starting one's study with a definition which makes the work *a priori* and biased toward one system of truth. Beginning with a functional definition will not do that, and not beginning with an explicit definition will not save one from it. The difference is not with the mere use of a definition, but with the kind of definition which is being used. Bleeker indicated that the historian of religions does begin with a definition even though it is vague, hardly formulated, and intuitive. If whatever implicit definition he operates under is treated as a 'real definition', i.e. as a statement (implicit or explicit, vague or clear, defined or intuited) that gives the 'essence' of the thing religion, then one is assuming that all the applications of 'religion' are univocal. If one operates under these conceptions he is positing a 'real definition' under an essential-intuitional method, whether stated or not. This is our argument about Eliade's phenomenology of symbolism.[58] On the other hand, if one utilizes a functional definition, one does not opt for any given truth system even if he explicitly states the definition at the beginning of his work. Functional definitions are neither true nor false.

By placing such a premium on category formation we are not underestimating the importance of familiarity with or analysis of historical data. The logician can content himself with the logical structures of knowledge without concern for the phenomena. The historian of religions must also concern himself with the logical structures of the knowledge he purports to acquire. He must familiarize himself with the definitional problem – a task he has not yet done. But he does so as preliminary to his real goal of accurately examining and presenting the data in response to the religious question.

To know that religio-historical categories are functional definitions is not to understand the phenomena. However, such definitions are *preparatory* to such understanding, and it is difficult to see how such understanding could be achieved until our use of terms is clarified. Anything less takes the historian of religions out of the academic and makes his work part of a religious experience. It is not that we do not have an intuitive notion of what words mean, which enables even the inarticulate to communicate somewhat. The point is that these intuitive meanings are often in conflict. The categories do not suffer from a lack of meaning, but from an overabundance of meaning which makes the word ambiguous. The definitional process involves clarifying what meaning or meanings we will permit the words to have in academic study.

The categories of longitude and latitude do not guarantee that the geographer will understand the cartographical features of the earth, but they enable him to discuss those features. The categories are valid to the extent to which they enable him to do so. If the categories make it impossible for him to relate to the phenomena that he finds, then they are inappropriate and ought to be changed.

This distinction between the nature of functional definitions and truth assertions about things shows how it is possible to answer certain questions which could not *on principle* be answered under the essential-intuitional method. The first question is whether the teachings of Confucius or the Buddha are 'religious'. Such a question cannot be answered merely by the definitional route, nor by a mere examination of the relevant data. Once one has offered a functional definition of religion, he can examine the data in each case to see if it fits the category of religion. The answer will depend upon what the data reveals, to be sure, but also upon the meaning one decides to give to the word 'religion'. If either procedure is ignored the question is in principle unanswerable.

Another question attempts to determine the relationship between religion and magic. It is just as well that this question has been abandoned, since on essential-intuitional principles the question is insoluable. Both terms are ambiguous. Having stipulated functional definitions of both 'religion' and 'magic', an examination of the relevant data will make an answer possible. The relationship between the realities so named may vary from culture to culture. But since both are functional definitions they are neither true nor false – and that goes for 'magic' as well as for 'religion'. But again, if either the definitional procedure or an examination of data is neglected, the question is in principle unanswerable.

Religio-historical categories, then, are functionally defined. In the next chapter we will turn to a functional definition of religion.

The Category of Religion

Having indicated the nature of category formation, we turn to an application of the functional-definitional principle to the category of 'religion'. There is no point in eliminating the use of the word 'religion' simply because it is ambiguous or has been reified, as has been suggested by Wilfred Cantwell Smith. Most of our words are ambiguous and many have been reified. The task before us is to offer a functional definition of 'religion' which will serve to indicate the limits of applicability of our method and to indicate the level on which we shall ask our questions of the available data.

While there is no reason to avoid general usage in assigning a meaning to the word 'religion', there is no cogent reason for seeking to stay close to popular usage either. We have argued that the word religion is ambiguous. Any functional definition will eliminate that ambiguity. What we are looking for is a definition which is also useful, that is, which enables us to ask the kind of question which we choose to ask.[1]

The category of religion is probably the most basic for the historian of religions. How he defines the word will determine the level on which his research and teaching will be conducted. While the offering of a functional definition of religion is not the end of the methodological question for the historian of religions, how this word is defined will determine that for which the historian of religions is looking. Furthermore, it will, of logical necessity, determine the usefulness or uselessness of certain other categories in arriving at that end. That is, the functional definition of religion is for the historian of religions an indication of his scholarly end.[2]

Since, in the light of the nature of functional definitions, there is no point in indicating what makes the 'best' definition, we will content ourselves with offering a functional definition of religion after which we will indicate how such a definition would operate in the history of religions.

A. FUNCTIONAL DEFINITION OF RELIGION

Religion is *ultimate concern*. I am here adopting the *terminology* of Paul Tillich. Tillich's definition is that 'Religion, in the largest and most basic sense of the word, is ultimate concern'.[3] But Tillich assigns a meaning to the words which I do not care to follow. He holds that both the subjective apprehension (concern) and the objective reality (ultimate) are implied when one sees religion as ultimate concern. One might point out that 'ultimate' merely modifies 'concern' thereby indicating its importance, and that it does not necessarily require equal attention with the objective reference which is better expressed with the phrase 'Ultimate Reality'. One need not deny the reality of the objective point of reference in any given ultimate concern, but, as we will point out later, investigation of that objective reality is not itself a part of historical research.

By 'ultimate' I do not intend to emphasize the metaphysical or the *object*(s) of ultimate concern. At the same time I do not intend to *deny* the objective reality. Neither affirmation nor denial is either necessary or desirable for historical research. By 'ultimate' I am referring to a concern which is *more important than anything else in the universe for the person involved.*[4] As William A. Christian states it:

> Then, on this theory, someone is religious if in his universe there is some-
> thing to which (in principle) all other things are subordinated. Being
> religious means having an interest of this kind. A belief is a religious belief if
> it is about something taken in this way. A feeling is a religious feeling if it
> is a response to something taken in this way. An overt action is a religious
> action if it is expressive or symptomatic of something taken in this way.[5]

Hence the study of religion will include the study of the ultimate concerns of persons and communities as well as the subordinate phenomena which are significantly related to such concerns. If the focus of the history of religions is ultimate concern, then the religious dimension of subordinate ideas, symbols, rites, etc., must all be understood in the light of their relation to ultimate concern. If some rite or symbol is only peripherally related to the ultimate concern of a person or community, its importance in the study of the religion of that person or community is negligible. A rite that has been religiously significant to one person or group may lose its religious significance for another and hence cease to qualify as a valid object of religious inquiry at that point.

B. IMPLICATIONS OF THIS FUNCTIONAL DEFINITION

Having indicated the meaning of the word 'religion', we will now inquire what such a functional definition means for historical inquiry.

First, the study of religion as ultimate concern is the study of man. It is perfectly legitimate to make the object of one's study God, Ultimate Reality, the Ground of Being, or Dharmakāya. But the object of historical study is the study of man and not the study of any of these. The historian is certainly interested in Śankara's or Gaudapāda's view of non-dual Reality, Tillich's Ground of Being, the view of Buddha in the *Lankāvatāra Sūtra*. But, historically speaking, these are all men's views of Ultimate Reality. While it is undoubtedly true that all views of Ultimate Reality are human in the sense that it is men who hold them, to ask 'What is the nature of Ultimate Reality'? is a different level question from 'What is Śankara's view of Ultimate Reality'? The former is a normative question while the latter is an historical question. The object of the former question centers on acquiring a knowledge of Ultimate Reality; the latter centers on acquiring a knowledge of Śankara. Hence the former is not a legitimate historical-level question while the latter surely is.

By defining religion as ultimate concern rather than Ultimate Reality, we have a definition that is historically useful in a way that ontologically-oriented definitions are not. If one defines religion as man's response to the Sacred, a prior theological or ontological understanding of 'the Sacred' is required. Without this it is futile to try to determine if men are responding to it. Such a definition takes us out of the realm of history and offers a definition which history cannot handle. To historicize the definition by intending what man has taken as the Sacred would place us within the realm of historical inquiry, but would require a functional definition of the Sacred so that it could be historically identified.[6] A definition which will be functional for historical study must center on the subject rather than on the object. This is not to ignore the various objects of ultimate concern which men have had. But the truth question is avoided on this level since the investigation centers on man and his concerns whether they might be deemed theologically legitimate or not.

Tillich enters the debate as to whether 'religion is here considered as a creative element of the human spirit rather than as a gift of divine revelation'.[7] This is a proper theological question. But it is not a question that is relevant to historical knowledge. When we state that the history of religions is the study of man rather than the study of God we are making a methodological stipulation and not a theological proposal. We are simply indicating that historical investigation is limited to the study of man. Neither theological assertion – 'religion is a creative element of the human spirit' or 'religion is a gift of divine revelation' – is in conflict with this *methodological* proposal. The reason is clear. The two statements (methodological and theological) are of different orders and hence cannot come in conflict. The functional definition that religion is what concerns men ultimately, then, enables us to clarify the nature of the religious question in the study of man and his history.

Some clarification is necessary regarding the place at which values enter into the history of religions. In the next chapter we will consider whether the values of the historian relativize his entire study. Here we are interested in the implications of the hope that the history of religions will contribute to a 'New Humanism'.[8] The history of religions is rich in describing the values which men have held in varying historical and cultural contexts. It is free (or should be) of commending any of these values for acceptance. The ultimate value of a belief or rite depends on its truth and that is a normative question. When religio-historical works recommend, either explicitly or by implication, the value of others for our approval, and buttress these with descriptively true statements about those who hold them, we have at best a pseudo-theology. One is free to make such recommendations, but they will be accepted by critically-minded persons only to the degree to which they are appropriately supported. And, to support values or theological assertions with descriptive statements, however true, is to offer assertions on one level (the normative) with evidence from another level (historical).

Second, religion as the ultimate concerns of men can be investigated on two levels – that of the ideal and that of observable realities. The recognition that religio-historical study involves two levels is not the result of our specific definition. This is a problem necessitated by the data we study and cannot be ignored without incurring objectionable consequences. The tendency of the believer is to identify his position in terms of the ideal, while the tendency of the outsider is to identify religion in terms of empirical realities. Identifying religion as ultimate concern enables one to take into consideration both the testimony of the believer as well as the empirical data which may clash with that testimony. It is then legitimate to identify ultimate concern on two levels:

(1) the thought systems which are explicitly constructed or merely implied by which men indicate what they believe should be of ultimate concern, and (2) the empirical indications of what in fact is ultimate in the lives of men regardless of what they profess. Apologetic concerns have sometimes emphasized the empirical realities (particularly when looking at others), while an undue acceptance of the witness of the believer has turned not a few books into sentimentality. Both the theoretical ideal and the empirical reality are part of the data, and an adequate methodology must be able to deal with both levels. On the theoretical level the study of religion will ascertain what theologies, rites, temples, etc., should mean if they are to be understood in terms of their intentions. There is always the possibility that the real and the ideal could approximate each other in certain persons or communities, but the likelihood of a gap existing between the real and the ideal is considerable. The study of religions always encounters these two levels. An adequate methodology must proceed with a functional definition which does not blur such a distinction.

Third, religion as ultimate concern is functional for the study of individuals and communities. Once the distinction is drawn between the ideal and the empirical, it becomes possible to handle the religious systems of individuals and communities alike. Both express themselves ideally in terms of that about which they think men *should* be ultimately concerned (even themselves) and that which *is actually determinative* in their lives. This is no less true of religious communities than of religious persons. Religious communities articulate creedal pronouncements, offer statements of faith, operate under principles of incorporation, or specify specific rites. The extent to which such are believed and/or practiced by the members (formal or informal) of the community is quite another matter.

Not all institutions are religious communities. A religious community is a body of persons who share an ultimate concern – at least on the ideal level, and possibly on the empirically real level. Religious communities tend to become organizations after a few generations when the original spirit or intent becomes less vital and cohesive. Hence there are religious communities, but they are less gross than we have been accustomed to think.[9] While there are indeed religious communities, it makes little sense to talk about 'the Christian community' or 'the Muslim community'. Regardless of certain continuities which exist in such designations, in each case one can find those for whom God or Nirvāṇa is ultimate and also those for whom the nation is ultimate and

'God' is dead. But even organizations (groups in which the members do not have a common ultimate concern) make religious pronouncements. These can be taken seriously for historical study on the ideal level, which simply means that the organization believes it would be good if its members believed or acted in a certain way even though sociological and psychological studies show that they do not.

It does appear that Wilfred Cantwell Smith has made a point. Religious study must begin with the individual. Religious study is not exhausted in the individual, but any study which begins with the phenomena must begin there. To be sure, even categories referring to the person might be historically misleading unless care is taken. It may be necessary to use the qualifiers 'early' and 'later' when referring to the theological work of Karl Barth. When persons have written enough or changed enough we may be forced to speak in such terms. This is not the result of the method or the definition, but the result of the complexity of the data which the method is able to reveal rather than to conceal. But, unless we begin with the individual we are unable to account for the religion of some men.

> If one takes the community as a prime concept in one's attempt to under-stand man's story, one cannot reckon with a social rebel in the name of the Lord like Amos, or with a hermit or forest dweller, or with an in-novator like Jesus or Muhammad from whom communities arise. Nor, for that matter, can one reckon with the modern man who feels his way toward a faith but adheres to no community, or who belongs to one community but finds his faith not confined within it; the Presbyterian who reads Methodist books, the Methodist who reads Buber or the Bhagavad Gita, the Muslim who is a sincere Indian nationalist, and, indeed any religious man who sees the value of human brotherhood. Further, one cannot understand the situation in China, where, as we have seen, the compartmentalization of men into boundried religious communities each around one religious tradion, or Western pattern, hardly obtains.[10]

C. POSSIBLE OBJECTIONS TO THIS DEFINITION

It remains for us to anticipate certain possible objections to our functional definition of religion as ultimate concern.

A *first* objection might be that some persons or groups do not have any ultimate concern as it has been defined. In response to such an objection, it should be said that there are probably not as many such cases as might at first be expected. It is necessary to distinguish between explicit and implicit ultimate concerns. There are those persons or groups who consciously and deliberately ask the religious question of themselves, and there are those who do not. When the latter is the case, this does not mean that the persons involved are any less religious, for there may be an ultimate concern which dominates their life style. Often the religious question will be answered with difficulty because of religious instability (the tendency to frequent religious changes in given persons), or because one does not know the subject of inquiry well enough by reason of insufficient data. But to conceed that one does not have sufficient data to answer the religious question in all instances or to recognize religious instability is not to say that in such cases the religious question is in principle unanswerable.

One must admit that the use of a functional definition such as has been offered does not guarantee that one will always come up with an answer to the religious question. Whatever one might expect, it is *in principle* possible to find some persons and certainly some groups that are not religious. If we offer ultimate concern as a functional definition of religion, we are not saying that everyone has it,[11] or that we will always find that for which we are looking, but that we are looking for this *when it can be found*. There must exist the possibility that some persons or some group will not yield an answer to the religious question. The *reason* for that is not significant for *historical* study. Whether it is because some people are non-religious or simply because the data necessary for discovering their religious answer is lacking may be monumental for the theologian, but it is irrelevant for the historian. However, historical investigation does demand that there remain the possibility that the religious question cannot always be answered. This points to the tentative nature of history.

Such a definition does not necessitate that the historian of religions impose patterns of ultimate concern where they do not exist. All historical study proceeds on the assumption that the investigator is honest and open to revision. When one operates under a functional definition he concedes that he is not searching for normative truth and that concession makes such honesty even more likely. One cannot deny that some historians of religions may force material into preconceived forms. But the problem is a *human* one, and is not dictated by the functional-definitional method, nor by the definition offered. It can happen as easily without a specified definition, and then it is less detectable. One does not disqualify a method because someone is not willing to abide by the rules of academic honesty, for such an unwillingness will lead *any* method to ruin.

Finally, one must accept the possibility of *religious ambiguity*. Not all persons or groups are systematic, either explicitly or implicitly. Hence they are religiously ambiguous. But this is not the result of the method. It is inherent in the data. One would only concede religious ambiguity as a last resort. By offering a functional definition of religion, the word is rendered unambiguous. Hence, when ambiguity appears, we know that it is not verbal ambiguity. The ambiguity resides in the person or group being studied. This method, then, enables us to identify religious ambiguity and to describe the nature of the ambiguity in certain cases. This itself can be an exciting historical investigation. To indicate a religious consistency and continuity as we have often done in the past is neither instructive nor useful when it is not true to the data. In the above manner, we are at least enabled to admit religious ambiguity where it does appear. But the admission of religious ambiguity is always a last resort. In historical study, we do not usually say that a thinker being studied is inconsistent until all attempts to understand him as consistent or in terms of development have failed.

A *second* objection to religion as ultimate concern might be that the definition is too broad. It could necessitate the study of nationalism, missile defense systems, and the stock market, in addition to 'Vaiṣṇavism', 'Śaivism', and 'Shinto'. This objection may have several levels of meaning. One possible meaning to this objection is that there are some 'religious' things that are left out of the definition while other 'non-religious' things are included. Such an objection must be rejected since it is based on the essential-intuitional method already dealt with in chapter one. The word 'religion' is ambiguous in common and scholarly usage, and a functional definition simply eliminates that ambiguity by assigning one meaning to the word. Hence a functional definition cannot be too broad or too narrow, particularly not on essentialist grounds. The word carries whatever meaning has been assigned to it. This objection often rests on the assumption that the word 'religion' is unambiguous. This we have shown to be false.

This objection might also mean that the definition does not suit the investigator since it does not allow him to do what *he* wants to do. Such an objection must be respected, but it does not throw doubt upon the definition itself. It merely points to the fact that different historians prefer to ask different questions. We have not suggested that the functional definition of religion as ultimate concern is the only legitimate functional definition of religion. One can only argue in that manner on essential-intuitional grounds. It can be contended, however, that this definition allows the present investigator to ask the question of the historical data that he chooses to ask and that other scholars might be interested in this question as well. While it is not an argument for defining religion in this manner, one might also point out that the ultimate concerns of men are *at least* one of the most important human questions that can be asked. It is difficult to maintain that what is of ultimate concern to men is not an important human question. Indeed, it is sufficiently important that if the historian of religions refuses to ask what matters have been of ultimate concern to men, then someone else should.

With religion as ultimate concern we must get used to admitting that there are no such things as purely religious data. There are only *data* of which we ask the *religious question*. Those data can include temples, beliefs, rites, defense systems, economic systems, artistic representations, political movements, etc. There is probably nothing which is immune to the religious. This is recognized by Eliade, who is proceeding under quite a different methodology than the one I am here proposing.

We must get used to the idea of recognizing hierophanies absolutely everywhere, in every area of psychological, economic, spiritual and social life. Indeed, we cannot be sure that there is *anything* – object, movement, psychological function, being or even game – that has not at some time in human history been somewhere transformed into a hierophany.... It is quite certain that anything man has ever handled, felt, come in contact with or loved *can* become a hierophany. We know, for instance, that all the gestures, dances and games children have, and many of their toys, have a religious origin – they were once the gestures and objects of worship. In the same way musical and architectural instruments, means of transport (animals, chariots, boats and so on) started by being sacred objects, sacred activities.... In the same way too, every trade, art, industry and technical skill either began as something holy, or has, over the years, been invested with religious value. This list could be carried on to include man's everyday movements (getting up, walking, running), his various employments (hunting, fishing, agriculture), all his physiological activities (nutrition, sexual life, etc.); perhaps too the essential words of the language, and so on.[12]

If one is willing to study sacred spears and stones in archaic cultures, it is absurd to suggest that it is illegitimate to consider the religious significance of nationalism or defense systems for modern man. Religious symbols must be expected to differ in diverse cultural settings. Some may see the secular city as a good to be embraced while others may make the theological judgment that it illustrates the fall of man, but for the contemporary historian of religions to deny that it is the religion of numerous of his contemporaries is absurd. Eliade finds it legitimate to analyze the religious dimensions in the popularity of *Planète*, Teilhard de Chardin, and Claude Lévi-Strauss.

My purpose here is more modest. I will try to see whether a historian of religions can decipher some hidden meanings in our so-called cultural fashions, taking as examples three recent vogues.[13]

One can study a temple, for example, on several levels, none of which exhausts the meaning of the temple. The art historian may be interested in its structural symmetry, the economist may inquire as to its finances and its role in the economy of the area, the political scientist may research its function in political protest movements. The historian of religions will be interested in the answers to all these levels of investigation. But his distinct contribution will be the religious one: how does the structure and use of the temple reflect the ultimate concern of those who built it and those who use it? His question does not exhaust the reality any more than do the others, but it is a significant question that is worth asking.

While the religious dimension is potentially as extensive as human culture, and while the study of religion is potentially of equal extent, it *need not* always be so. Practically speaking it is not always possible or desirable to cast one's net so wide. What is being offered is not the command that historians of religions henceforth study bridges, missile systems, and stock markets. This is a *method* for examining these things or even some of those systems and rites which have been more commonly considered religious. One may choose to limit his discussion to the thought of Vallabha or Muhammad Iqbal if he chooses, but a religious study would ask the question of ultimacy and how the other facets of their thought relate to that ultimate concern. Others may choose to consider the religious dimensions of culture that have in the modern world been considered secular. Such a definition may indeed modify the type of data that will be considered in religious study, but *even more important* it will determine *how* whatever data we *do* consider will be handled. Hence the question of ultimacy can be asked of anything in principle, even though in practice it might not.

A third objection might be that such a definition is merely the extension of one's personal experience.

> Those scholars, for example Baird, who assume that religious values are ultimate often extrapolate from their own personal experience and, in so doing, also assume that *homo religiosus* is the essential definition of man. Ultimacy is clearly a value category and cannot be justified other than in an authoritarian fashion.[14]

Helfer confuses the nature of functional definitions. He is operating under the all too common essential-intuitional method. He assumes that there is such a thing as 'religion' and that one is imposing a self-valued essence on it. But that is to confuse the nature of functional definitions. A functional definition is not an extension of a metaphysical position on available data. It is merely a declaration of how one intends to use a word and in that sense indicates the type of question which will be asked of the data. Helfer has 'real definition' in mind when he offers the criticism on ultimacy. He assumes that we are defining a thing rather than a word, for that is the only way that one could be guilty of extending his experience to the universe. One's decision to use religion in a certain way is not to say anything about the nature of things, but only about the applicability of a word. It is a pledge to use a word that way and hence is a functional definition.

Only if one assumes that the religious question exhausts the data does the definition posit a metaphysical point of view. If one merely indicates that he intends to ask that question whenever it is applicable, he is saying nothing about what is essential about the nature of man. He is merely indicating 'the limits of applicability, as well as the applicability, of a particular method'.[15] It is easy to turn any level of investigation into a metaphysical position. But by offering a functional definition one clearly indicates on which level he is operating and hence guards against the transformation of methodology into metaphysics.

3

The Category of History

Having indicated what we are searching for when we study religion, it is now necessary to indicate what is to be intended when we call this discipline the *history* of religions. It must be stated that the term 'history of religions', is not always used in its most obvious sense. This is because it has become an accepted translation of *Allgemeine Religionswissenschaft*.

In the English-speaking world the imposing title of 'General science of religions' has not been used widely, partly because it is too long and awkward, and partly because the English word 'science' tends to be misleading. Thus, the world-wide organization of scholars in this field has recently adopted an official English title, 'The International Association for the Study of the History of Religions.' It is readily apparent that the term 'history of religions' has come to be regarded as a synonym for the 'general science of religions', and as such the nature of the discipline must be discussed in the total context of *Religionswissenschaft*.[1]

It is sometimes held that the history of religions includes history, phenomenology of religion, sociology of religion, and psychology of religion. But it is further urged that the history of religions is not merely an umbrella under which these otherwise independent disciplines find shelter. This, it would seem, is a necessary inference if one is to say that the history of religions is a discipline at all. Hence it is also distinguished from these other methods. 'Actually, it is only one among many different approaches, such as philosophy of religion, psychology of religion, sociology of religion, and theology.'[2]

But if this is the case, then the history of religions is not merely a 'general science of religions'. It must be conceived as a distinct method with a distinct goal. But how is it to be defined and how is it to be placed in relation to the other disciplines mentioned? It is Kitagawa's view that the history of religions is not normative like theology and philosophy of religion in that it does not offer proposals for belief.

Unlike philosophy of religion and theology, however, the history of religions does not 'endorse' any particular system offered by the diverse religions of the world, nor does it advocate, as many ultra-liberals think it ought, any new universal synthetic religion.[3]

On the other hand, the history of religions is not merely a descriptive discipline such as anthropology or sociology.

Our thesis is that the discipline of *Religionswissenschaft* lies between the normative disciplines on the one hand and the descriptive disciplines on the other. Following Wach, we may divide *Religionswissenschaft* into historical and systematic subdivisions. Under the heading of 'historical' come the general history of religion and the histories of specific religions. Under the heading of 'systematic' come phenomenological, comparative, sociological, and psychological studies of religions. All these subdivisions are regarded as integral parts of *Religionswissenschaft* or the history of religions, in the way we use this term.[4]

Kitagawa also indicates that the term 'history of religions means different things to different people'.[5] One sometimes senses that there is an effort afoot to perform the impossible – to unite into *one discipline* what various people have included under the rubric of 'history of religions'. Hence, following Wach, Kitagawa is willing to place sociology and psychology of religions as well as phenomenology of religion as part of the 'systematic subdivision' of the history of religions. But if the history of religions is actually *a discipline* then it must have a distinct *methodology*. To the extent to which it is *a distinct method*, to that extent it is unable to include sociological and psychological studies of religion as 'subdivisions'. To the extent that it does do this in the above manner, to that extent it ceases to be *a distinct discipline* and becomes a mere way of organizing other disciplines under a larger convenient rubric. Now the problem which this scheme has is inherent and hence insoluble. It wants to maintain that the history of religions, while not the only way of studying religions, is a distinct way. On the other hand, it wants to include these other methods as 'subdivisions'.[6]

That the history of religions cannot isolate itself from other disciplines is obvious enough, and that we depend on the work of others is also clear. But what makes a discipline is not the examination of a specific subject matter, but the exercise of a specific method. This is why the urging of historians of religions that they represent an 'autonomous' discipline has not convinced those outside the camp.

Perhaps our present point can be made by a reference to Mircea Eliade's *Shamanism: Archaic Techniques of Ecstasy*.[7] In his Foreword this same inherent ambiguity is expressed. Eliade wants to maintain that the history of religions is 'another approach',[8] that it attempts to get at the religious meaning of the historically concrete hierophany by taking account of its transhistorical meaning, and that the strict 'historian' as well as the psychologist, sociologist, and ethnologist may well ignore such 'transhistorical meanings'.[9] On the other hand, it is again maintained that while not underestimating the significant contributions of these other disciplines, the historian of religions' 'mission is to integrate the results of ethnology, psychology, and sociology'.[10]

> In the last analysis, it is for the historian of religions to synthesize all the studies of particular aspects of shamanism and to present a comprehensive view which shall be at once a morphology and a history of this complex religious phenomenon.[11]

What Eliade offers, however, is not a *synthesis*. It is *a different approach* since he does not synthesize what is offered through these approaches, particularly what is most distinctive about them. Instead, he selects those things in such works which are useful for the question *he* is asking. Hence, although it is to be expected that the psychologist would interpret the shaman in terms of a 'psych in crisis' and see it in terms of some kind of mental disease, Eliade rejects the analysis of mental illness while accepting that the 'shamanic vocation is manifested by a crisis, a temporary derangement of the future shaman's spiritual equilibrium'.[12] The sociologist's analysis of the social function of the shaman is not retained as a methodological approach, but it is utilized merely to 'reinforce the element of human and historical concreteness'.[13] Although the ethnologist's analysis accentuates this concreteness, Eliade moves beyond this method when he recognizes that the historian of religions must give attention to the transhistorical religious meaning of any given hierophany while the ethnologist need not do so.

This means that Eliade is not *synthesizing* the results of all these types of studies. He is simply using what he finds there that is relevant for answering his question. He is ignoring some aspects of their studies, rejecting others, and transcending others in answer to a new methodological question. Such a procedure need not deny the value of these other methodologies, but it would be futile to try to bring them under a single methodological umbrella simply because one finds significant insights and useful information in such books. In Eliade's approach, ethnology, psychology of religion, sociology of religion are hardly 'subdivisions' of the general history of religions. They simply contain valuable information that any historian of religions can hardly ignore. But so do many other books. The process is clearly selective and that selection is determined by the distinct method of Eliade's 'history of religions' and not by the distinct methodologies of ethnology, psychology, or sociology. It is simply not possible to ask the functional, psychological, and religious questions of the data *simultaneously*.

We have argued that in the case of ambiguous words, a functional definition is appropriate, not to prejudge reality, but to stipulate the meanings of the words we apply to that reality. Kitagawa has a perfect right to use the phrase 'history of religions' as he chooses. But the arbitrary aspect of functional definitions does not permit the inclusion of contradictory elements. The arbitrary nature means that any word can be used to refer to any thing, not that we can be contradictory in our use of words. Hence it is not communicative to say that such 'disciplines' are 'subdivisions' of the systematic branch of the history of religions *and also* to say that the 'history of religions' is a 'distinct discipline'. In this case the 'subdivisions' are not aspects of a total method, but are distinct methods themselves. To the extent to which they become aspects of the distinct method of the history of religions, to that extent they lose their own distinctiveness and hence are not included in their prior disciplinary integrity. There is a difference between a religious and a sociological question since the first centers on the question of ultimacy while the second centers on society and asks what functions ultimate concerns fill in society. It is equally true that there is a difference between the historical question and the phenomenological one.

In order to deal with that in the next chapter it becomes necessary to this one to indicate what we mean by *history*. Even in Kitagawa's schema, a distinction is conceded between the 'historical' and the 'systematic' branches of this supposed discipline. If that be the case we are responsible for defining the limits of historical treatment.

A. THE MEANING OF 'HISTORY'

My functional definition of history is that history is *the descriptive study of the human past*. History is not the study of God or Ultimate Reality. That must remain the task of theology. Hence, historical study cannot be the study of 'the Sacred'. History limits itself to the study of man. To the extent to which history is interested in natural phenomena, these are only supportive for the basic historical question – which is a human one.

History begins to be interested in the past when human beings first appear in it. Its essential concern is with human experiences and actions. It is true, of course, that history records not merely what human beings did and suffered, but also a considerable number of *natural* events in the past – earthquakes, floods, droughts and the like. But its interest in these events is strictly subsidiary. The historian is not concerned, at any point of his work, with nature for its own sake; only with nature as a background to human activities. If he mentions natural events, it is because those events had effects on the lives of men and women whose experiences he is describing. Had they no such effects he would not have mentioned them.[14]

Any thought or activity relating to man is the proper object of historical research. Given the immensity of the human past, we have generally divided our energies. This is necessary and legitimate. The only danger is that once one gets absorbed in a limited area he will forget that the historical quest has been divided and that all we have is a portion. It is possible to study the human past in terms of art history, economics, philosophical systems, political arrangements, etc., etc. We have chosen to limit our study of history to the religious question, that is, what has been and is of ultimate concern to men as individuals and in community.

The present functional definition of religion is now clearly seen to be quite appropriate for historical study. Some definitions center on Ultimate Reality, a topic which is worth pursuing, but which cannot be pursued within the confines of history as here defined. If history limits itself to man, then the historical study of religion must operate with a definition which history can handle. By defining religion as ultimate concern, we have centered the matter in man, without implying by such a *functional definition* any *normative* judgment about either man or God.

History is a temporal study. It attempts to locate religion in its cultural setting, and to reveal sequential connections. Furthermore, history is descriptive. Historical study attempts to describe the human past accurately, not to pronounce about it. History is not concerned to tell which views men have held are true or false and which are most worthy of allegiance. It does not pass moral judgments on the actions of men; it merely gives an accurate description of what they were. It might tell us some of the historical consequences of human actions and also some of their historical conditions, but to state that these consequences are desirable or undesirable for man places one outside of the descriptive discipline. This means that although religion is ultimate concern, the historical study of religion will not *of itself* add anything to one's own ultimate concern. Admittedly, history has numerous uses. The historical study of religion may be useful in constructing a viable religious position. A theologian would be rather poorly prepared if he did not have accurate knowledge of what previous theologians had said. But *to use* historical knowledge is to go *beyond history.*

Problem solving may be aided by a knowledge of man's past, but since it is *based on* history it is an *extension* which requires the intrusion of values and norms. This makes it more or less than history. We cannot deny that scholars who call themselves historians often go beyond history in our sense of the word. But we are offering a functional definition as a means toward the articulation of a method. We are not attempting to find some common 'essence' which will reveal some possible bond between all who call themselves 'historians'. It seems clear that the word 'history' is lexically ambiguous. However one wants to say it, one can never arrive at metaphysical truth or moral truth from a descriptive study of the past. For clarity of thought, we prefer to use 'history' to refer to a purely descriptive method. The extent to which this is achieved or the extent to which it is even possible will have to be raised shortly. But, as descriptive, the historical study of religion cannot itself be religious without its ceasing to be historical. Historical study merely describes the human past. It does not indicate what should be espoused, or how man should live.

Some uses of the word 'history' make it synonymous with philosophy.[15] Such is the tendency of those whose theories of historical knowledge have been engulfed by idealistic philosophy. This view is found in R. G. Collingwood and has found its way into religious history to a considerable extent.[16]

We prefer to distinguish between these two scholarly activities. Not infreqeuntly the failure to do so makes for bad philosophy and theology while at the same time it dissolves history. To say that history is the same as philosophy is like saying that all knowledge is historical. Such a statement, if thoroughly followed, threatens to dissolve all knowledge of the past.

History, then, is itself penultimate, even when it is concerned with the study of ultimates.

> To me it seems that no historical investigation can provide either a philosophy, or a religion, or a substitute for religion. If in this I express only a personal opinion, I think I should have a general consensus of the working historians with me if I confined myself to the simpler conclusion that we work with limited aims. We try to find the truth about this or that, not about things in general. Our work is not to see life steadily and see it whole, but to see one particular portion of life right side up and in true perspective.[17]

Interjecting values or moral judgments into descriptions is also unhistorical. Here again mere documentary evidence is insufficient. Without appropriate theoretical support, such become pure assertions.

> The truth is that, as we have seen already, we need no help from the historian to bring us to the recognition of the criminality of religious persecution or wholesale massacre or the modern concentration camp or the repression of dissident opinions. And those who do not recognize that the killing and torturing of human beings is barbarity will hardly be brought to that realization by any labels and nicknames historians may attach to these things.[18]

There is no point to objecting that some 'historians' do not fit into this definition of history. Such an objection is based upon the essential-intuitional method which is no more valid for defining history than it was for defining religion. We do not deny that there have been numerous lexical definitions of history and that history departments operate in this regard with as much latitude as religion departments. They either allow various functional definitions of history to exist together in friendly (or unfriendly) competition, or they simply operate without a functional definition at all. I am not telling either camp how they should organize their departments, but am attempting to set up a series of functional definitions that will enable the historian of religions to deal with what scholars are logically able to do – whether or not a given scholar in a given department does more than one thing.

There is no reason why it is necessary to force scholars into artificial disciplinary categories without overlap. But there is good reason for such logical clarification so that even if one follows more than one procedure, he knows the limits of each and how each operates. Such will not restrain the 'historian' from making theological statements. But it should point the error of supporting them with descriptively true statements.

The history of religions, then, is a description of the ultimate concerns of men and communities in the past (including the immediate past which we sometimes mistakenly call the present). The historical study of religions does not mean studying the 'historical religions' as a 'wholeness'.[19] The history of religions involves the attempt to study the ultimate concerns of persons and communities in their historical givenness, ascertaining how subordinate things and penultimate matters relate to that most important concern reflected in their thought (ideal level) and or in their lives (empirical level).

The chronological aspect of history enters at numerous places, not the least in tracing the innumerable cases of religious change. Religious change is treated historically by indicating how certain matters which are penultimate or subordinate for some person or group achieves ultimacy for another. No one thing or concern can forever be considered religious. This is the way it is with men of whom history is the study. The method is not responsible for such change, it merely reveals how complex the data are.

Perhaps an illustration from the *Kaṭha Upaniṣad* will clarify my point. Naciketas is given three boons by Yama, god of death. The first two boons pose no problem, but for the third boon he requests an answer to the question of what happens to a man when he dies. Trying to dissuade Naciketas, Yama offers an attractive substitute.

> Choose centenarian sons and grandsons,
> Many cattle, elephants, gold, and horses.
> Choose a great abode of earth.
> And thyself live as many autumns as thou desirest.
> This, if thou thinkest as equal boon,
> Choose – wealth and long life!
> A great one on earth, O Naciketas, be thou.
> The enjoyer of thy desires I make thee.[20]

Yama is offering a gift which would have satisfied the man whose concerns are reflected in the *Ṛgveda*. Apart from the late hymns which are more inclined to philosophical probing, man's ultimate concern seemed to be centered on precisely these matters. How could one have a long life, with health, wealth, and sons, and then go to abide with the deities at death. The sacrifices were offered to influence the favorably disposed deities to assist in this direction. But the religion of Naciketas is different. He will not settle for such a grant because there is something that is more important to him. The content of ultimacy has changed. His reply to Yama begins with the two words: 'Ephemeral things'. He will not be satisfied until Yama answers *his* question.

Then Yama enters into a discussion of the nature of ignorance and the indestructable Ātman. This religious motif becomes more common in the Upanisadic literature. The means toward this ultimate concern is no longer sacrifice as in the *Ṛgveda*. The means is now meditation. Hence the religious end *and* the religious means have changed.

Such is not always the case. Sometimes the end is the same while the means differs. In Śankara's *advaita vedānta*, in the Pāli tradition, and in the thought of Nāgārjuna, the goal is freedom, release, *mokṣa*, or *Nirvāṇa*. In each case ultimacy is seen in terms of a non-dual (and therefore indescribable) experience. However, the means in the Pāli canon is through analysis of phenomena into *skhandhas*, *dhātus*, and *āyatanas*, and through meditating on the fact of universal change. Śankara also emphasizes meditation although he gives more place to bhakti as a preliminary practice which is finally superceded. But meditation for Śankara concentrates not so much on the impermanent as on the real or permanent. Nāgārjuna, on the other hand, uses the religious means of dialectic in which by reducing all views to absurdity, the Real (not another view of it) simply appears. In later Indian religious history persons whose religious zeal is nationalistically oriented (hence the end differs) will again use meditation, pūjā, and fasting as a religious means. The manner in which various persons and groups in differing situations elevate certain matters to ultimacy or subordinate other things to penultimacy is the study of the history of religions. In each case, of course, a careful inquiry into the religio-historical question will be much more detailed than the above cursory sketch might indicate.

The history of religions, then, is systematic in that it asks the religious question at various points in history. The religious question, involving ultimacy, involves a systematic answer. But it is also historical in that the answer is fully rooted in the cultural setting and is related to the shifting of the subordinate and the ultimate at various times and places. The history of religions is further historical in that it makes no attempt to give any more than an accurate description of the religious dimension of the human past.

B. IS RELIGIO-HISTORICAL KNOWLEDGE POSSIBLE?

I do not want to enter into a discussion as to whether *any* knowledge is possible. I will assume that it is. Those who disagree would presumably not be reading this book since they could not hope to learn anything. Nor would they be able to offer any valid arguments against my assumption without refuting themselves. Admittedly invalid statements could hardly invalidate the assumption that knowledge is possible. Even to reject the possibility of knowledge requires some knowledge. That is all that I want to assume.

The question to which we address ourselves at this point is whether *religio-historical* knowledge is possible? And, by religio-historical knowledge I mean accurate descriptions about man's religious past.

In a rather basic way the view that questions the possibility of accurate descriptions of the past is historical relativism. Historical relativism is the view that 'no historical work grasps the nature of the past (or present) immediately, that whatever 'truth' a historical work contains is relative to the conditioning processes under which it arose and can only be understood with reference to those processes'.[21]

Mandelbaum continues:

> Now the fact that every historical work, like my intellectual endeavor, is limited by psychological and sociological conditions (to mention only two) is indisputable. The radical novelty in historical relativism lies in the fact that it claims that the truth of the work, its meaning and validity, can only be grasped by referring its content to these conditions. In short, the relativist believes that to understand a history we must not only understand what is said in it but also why this is said.[22]

Mandelbaum adds that this is what philosophers have called the genetic fallacy.

If such a position were followed consistently, no valid knowledge of the past would be possible. This position holds that a knowledge of the past is always dependent not only upon what is said by the historian, but why and out of what context he said it. An infinite regress then becomes necessary: a third party is needed to analyze not only the analysis of the second, but also the context out of which it was made; and then the analysis which he makes is in turn made in some cultural context, and hence necessitates a fourth; and so on *ad infinitum*.

The following statement indicates clearly an important characteristic of historical relativism.

> In the first place the facts of history never come to us 'pure', since they do not and cannot exist in a pure form: they are always refracted through the mind of the recorder. It follows that when we take up a work of history, our first concern should be not with the facts which it contains but with the historian who wrote it.[23]

Carr is not speaking of some history or some facts. He says, 'the facts of history *never* come to us "pure"'; 'they do not and cannot exist is an "pure" form'; 'they are *always* refracted' (emphasis mine). The invalidity of the relativist position is not that it fails to describe something that *some* historians do or that it fails to describe that something accurately. The failure is that it universalizes the particular and states unequivocally that this is what *all* historians *must* do. When the case is stated in terms as boldly and universally as this, knowledge of the past is no longer possible. One might be tempted to suggest that we have access only to the historian through his works, but then the infinite regress makes even that impossible.

What, then, do we mean by historical objectivity? 'Where we are fully entitled to speak of the "objectivity" of a piece of knowledge, the knowing subject knows an object before him, independent of himself; the personality of the knower has no significance for the content of the piece of knowledge.... It thus claims to be valid in precisely the same manner for every subject'.[24] The ability to gain valid knowledge about the psychological processes of the historian is not denied, but that is another matter. Nor are we saying that such knowledge is never relevant to an understanding of what some historians write. It is, nevertheless, possible to know something about the past since a consideration of who claims to know this is *not always* a necessary consideration. We do not imply that all statements about the past can be descriptive or objective in this manner, but that *some can be*. This makes historical knowledge a possibility.

But, there are some questions which have been raised which seem to make objectivity or valid knowledge of the past impossible. We must consider a few such objections.

Theological and interpretive inevitability
The possibility of religio-historical knowledge has been thrown into question by Hendrik Kraemer in his attempt to justify a theological starting point for the study of man's religions. It is Kraemer's contention that the claim to be 'scientific' and 'objective' is nothing more than that – a claim. It has not been actualized nor can it be. The goal of 'understanding' cannot be achieved without 'interpretation'.

> To 'understand' or to 'comprehend' religion or a religion, we conclude, means to interpret it. Interpretation is not solely, nor even mainly, an intellectual but an existential activity. In regard to art this is readily acknowledged. In regard to religion it is easily forgotten, but nevertheless religion is *the* field in which it must be taken into account that man in all his activities, including his supposedly 'purely' intellectual activity, cannot escape his existential situation.[25]

Hence, while the so-called scientific study of religions may be a necessary historical reaction against the confinements of a rigid orthodoxy, it is not a possibility. Value-judgments inevitably enter into the study. Instead of approaching the 'Science of Religion' without prejudice *(voraussetzungslos)*, such scholars always operated under axiomatically accepted presuppositions *(Voraussetzungen)*.

> ...Underneath these 'scientific' attempts there are (for the most part unconscious) attitudes which are non-'scientific', i.e. elements of *Weltanschauung* in which there is contained a certain conception of man, life and the world, coupled with value-judgments which have non-scientific grounds and therefore cannot be regarded as universally valid verifications.[26]

This makes the theological approach to man's religions legitimate and inevitable. If one cannot help entering the normative realm, then he should do so openly. When one's presuppositions are placed in clear view, then the theologian 'can be free of a false make-believe of "scientific" objectivity'.[27]

Kraemer traces the history of the history of religions to show how the normative has entered into scholarly deliberations. According to Kraemer, Joachim Wach is particularly vulnerable. Wach emphasized the descriptive aspect of the history of religions and held that one should proceed without prejudice. The concept of epoché was brought into service as the 'studious attitude of avoiding judgments of value and truth'.[28] But Wach's goal of 'understanding' required too much to enable it to be 'scientific'.

> The simple consideration that this kind of *Verstehen* be pursued by Phenomenology, cannot be accomplished without real divination and congeniality, without a *verstehende Persönlichkeit* (an understanding mind), shows already that the total being of a scholar, which includes his subjectivity, is called into action.[29]

Kraemer's goal is not to plead for complete objectivity, but to offer a more scientific approach which means making one's theological assumptions explicit from the start.

Akin to Kraemer's theological inevitability is the elimination of historical knowledge by claiming that all statements about the past are interpretive. Descriptive statements are sometimes distinguished from interpretive ones. However, it is not uncommon to be told that all statements about the past involve interpretation. Part of the confusion lies in the usage of the word 'interpretation' as a synonym for 'judgment'. It is true that no descriptive statement can be made apart from the judgment of the historian, but to use the term 'interpretation' so broadly is confusing. If the word 'interpretation' is used to include all possible statements about the human past, then we are left with the need for another word to distinguish between levels of 'interpretation'.

One is making an interpretive statement about the past when that statement involves a level of meaning which requires verification from a method other than the mere citing of historical data. In his study of Henry VIII, J. C. Flugel has made so many interpretive statements that the work itself might be called interpretive.

> Nevertheless, we cannot but suppose that the difficulties and dangers which surrounded his father's throne must have exercised a powerful influence over the younger Henry's mind. The envy with which, even in ordinary families, a son is apt to look upon the superior power and privileges of a father is liable to be intensified when the father enjoys the exceptional influence and honor appertaining to a king. Under these circumstances any threat to the father's authority almost inevitably arouses in the son the idea of superseding the father.[30]

That difficulties attended the throne of Henry's father is something that can be verified or rejected according to historical method. The extent to which these difficulties could have influenced Henry's mind, the relationship of sons to fathers, and the psychological conditions under which a son might think of superseding his father, lead to statements which depend upon one's psychological point of view; and that discipline has its own methods of verification. What we have, then, is a set of statements of a psychological nature which are used to interpret another set of historical import. In such a case the verification of the statement in question is not a simple one of examining the historical data, because, even when that evidence is in, something remains for an adequate verification of the statement.

> Furthermore, this failure in the fertility of his marriage aroused superstitious fears connected with Henry's Oedipus complex. The idea of sterility as a punishment for incest is one that is deeply rooted in the human mind, and in the case of a union such as that of Henry and Catherine, there was scriptural authority for the infliction of a penalty of this description.[31]

Here we are introduced to the psychological judgment passed on a dead man who cannot even lie down upon our couch, that he had an Oedipus complex, and that incest is deeply rooted in the human mind as being punished by sterility. The footnote used to support that statement is not taken from any data that might substantiate the fact that Henry expressed such fears, but rather from a reference to Frazer's *Totemism and Exogamy*. The author says, in effect, since this is the way men are and this has been the case elsewhere with certain frequency, it must be characteristic of man and therefore also of Henry. The next statement is even more bold.

> It is true that Henry is reported to have himself denied the truth of this; but even if (as is very possibly the case) the rumor itself is exaggerated, it may well have been founded on some genuine attraction which Henry may have felt for the Lady Elizabeth. If this is so, in the light of psychoanalytic knowledge, it would appear not overbold to suggest that the mother and daughter, Elizabeth and Mary Blount, were, to Henry's unconscious mind, substitutes for Elizabeth and Mary Tudor – his mother and sister respectively.[32]

Here the author is bold enough to venture an interpretation (which is contrary to a report of Henry's own statement), probably based on the assumption that one's unconscious motivation is not always what one's language states. One further illustration will suffice.

Now there can be little doubt that Henry was a person whose Oedipus complex found expression in such a way. On this hypothesis it becomes possible to explain two very constant features of his love life; his fickleness (which tended to make him unable to love a woman, once his possession of her was assured) and the desire for some obstacle between him and the object of his choice. We shall come across sufficient examples of these, as we study the further course of his checkered conjugal career.[33]

This theory is based on Freud's analysis of love life which the author has used to interpret the available historical data.

Simply because a statement is interpretive does not make it valid or invalid. Interpretive statements cannot, by their nature be verified solely with historical evidence. Such statements can be valid, but the verification must be *both* historical *and* theoretical. Interpretive statements always rest on two poles. The biblical statement 'Christ died for our sins' is interpretive since it involves a theology.Theological interpretation is also legitimate, but then the statements depend not only on the probability of the historical aspect, but also on the validity of the theology involved.[34]

What is the difference, then, between an interpretive statement and a descriptive one? A descriptive statement is one which involves a level of meaning that can be verified by citing historical documentation. There are many statements which historians can make that are more significant than 'In the year 49 B. C. Caesar crossed the Rubicon' which are still of descriptive nature. This does not mean that all descriptive statements are of equal probability, but it does mean that they do not have imposed on them a level of meaning other than the historical. Descriptive statements, then, are dependent for their probability on the historical data available for their support.[35]

It remains possible to ask the religious question historically. One can grant with Kraemer that it is the total scholar who is at work in the historical study of religions. But the total man *need not always* ask the normative question. While he may not finally do justice to his own totality by not doing so, there are indeed other legitimate questions which are penultimate. The 'whole man' may ask questions and offer answers on various levels. One level (the normative) is: 'What value or truth does this expression contain?' Another (the historical) is: 'What is the expression and what does it mean to the one who uses it'?

There are levels which one might like to probe but which are presently beyond our reach. There are others, answers to which have only low degrees of probability or are mere possibilities because the data cannot answer the question as framed. It might be pointed out that using the Pāli canon to answer the religious question for the community which produced it will yield an answer with a much higher degree of probability than using the same body of literature to answer the religious question for Siddhārta Gautama.

There are those who are led to agree that descriptive statements about the past are not possible because of their tendency to ask what might be called low probability-yield questions. However interesting, some questions cannot be historically answered, and others cannot be answered because of sparsity of data or because the wrong kind of data exists for the question asked. Accurate knowledge of the past depends not so much upon the data available. This is what makes the questions about the historical Jesus or Siddhārta so difficult. One is asking of documents that admittedly preach a faith a question, the answer to which lies *behind* those documents. Most low probability-yield questions result from asking of data kinds of questions it is not intended to answer. To persist in asking such questions will hardly raise the degree of probability although it might raise one's psychological degree of certainty by sheer familiarity with the conjecture. One is sometimes confronted with the objection that it is not possible to say nothing, that one must offer a conjecture. Such a reply is absurd. It is not *necessary* to offer a conjecture. It is tempting and interesting to be sure, but not necessary. And the conjecture hardly adds much *valid knowledge* about the human past. One must mentally raise all possible meanings that the phallic emblems found in the Indus Valley excavations might have. But unless one is able to offer more than mere possibilities and conjectures, no real *knowledge* about man's religious past is added to our store. One need not deny the heuristic value of conjecture and asking apparently unanswerable questions of historical data. But the results must be at least probable to be considered valid knowledge about the past.

Ernst Benz asks a question which can be answered with some facility when he seeks to understand the nature of the polytheistic option in Shinto. But he introduces another realm when he asks: 'What attracts the wealthy can manufacturer of Kyoto to the shrine of the rice god Inari and causes him to donate whole pyramids of his cans and his pickles?'[36] And, when he asks: 'What moves a devout Hindu to pass by the Kali temple and the Vishnu temple one day, and hurry to the sanctuary of Krishna to offer him his sacrifice of flowers and his prayers and to participate the next day in the Kali festival?'[37] he is asking a question that is difficult enough to answer for one's own religion. At least this cannot be seen as merely being part of the question of the nature of the polytheistic option. It is an intensely personal question and an answer can be attempted on various levels of personal involvement itself.

All historical statements are generalizations

Carl Becker held that what we have called descriptive statements are really generalizations of many smaller facts.[38] This, he holds, is true of the statement 'In the year 49 B. C. Caesar crossed the Rubicon' and all other historical statements as well. Such a view tends to confuse the issue. Generalizations are statements which are based on other descriptive statements and summarize their implications. At least a generalization is 'a proposition that describes some attribute common to two or more objects'.[39] The Caesar statement is simply a descriptive statement about an event. That one could possibly make numerous other descriptive statements of greater or lesser import about the same event is simply to say that some events are sufficiently complex to allow numerous descriptive statements to be made about them. Not to make all descriptive statements about an event that might possibly be made does not make those statements that are made generalizations. From the realization that the historian cannot say everything about a given event even if he chooses to, that is, from the fact that the historian's knowledge is finite and not 'God's knowledge' it is often reasoned that what he says is less than accurate. This is not a necessary inference. That written history is less than complete should be obvious. But that one must say everything that could be said in order that anything that he might say about the past could be accurate, or that he must know everything in order to know anything must be rejected unless one is also willing to forfeit the possibility of *any knowledge at all*. Many descriptive statements about the past are highly probable and are therefore valid as long as one does not imply that they are more than they really are – a part. There is a profound difference between holding that one can make accurate statements about something and holding that because one can only make statements about *something* even those statements cannot be accurate. All statements, then, are not generalizations.

This also introduces the obvious point that if one cannot present any event in its entirety, then the statements he chooses to make have involved some element of selectivity. That selectivity takes place should be obvious enough. It is the implications that are sometimes drawn from such an admission that are unacceptable.

The first supposed implication is stated in the following way by Becker.

What is it that leads one historian to make out of all the possible true affirmations about a given event, certain affirmations and not others? Why, the purpose he has in mind will determine that.[40]

This is true, but the real question is whether the purpose he has in mind is a legitimate one given the data at his disposal. The issue is not that the historian exercises judgment, for that is part of an interesting psychological question. The question is whether or not his selection does violence to the data.[41] If we are going to support the notion that all selection does violence to the data, then we must also accept in that parcel the view that no knowledge of the past is possible.

Becker goes even further when he states that the purpose in the mind of the historian not only determines his selectivity but also imposes any meaning that the written history might have. 'The event itself, the facts, do not say anything, do not impose any meaning'.[42] One meaning of this assertion might be that the events themselves have no meaning until it is supplied by the historian. This consideration will be handled shortly when we deal with causal statements. If, on the other hand, this means that factual or descriptive statements have no meaning, it is absurd. They say whatever it is that they say – as is true of all adequately constructed sentences. There are different levels of meaning. To say that a descriptive statement means nothing is simply to say that one does not consider that level of meaning significant. Such may be correct, but it does not therefore add up to the elimination of all levels of meaning so that one can say that statements of fact have *no* meaning. The factual or descriptive statement, 'Indulgences were sold in Germany in 1517', is a descriptive statement which may not explain the existence of Protestantism until it is put in a context with other descriptive statements, but even alone it does mean something, namely that in 1517 in Germany indulgences actually were sold. A deeper meaning may not be available unless one includes a theological analysis of indulgences, but that is another matter. There are levels of meaning, and the statement exhibits one level of meaning even when it stands alone.

Becker's second implication of selectivity is the commonly heard one that the historian cannot eliminate the personal equation. This argument takes various forms among relativists, but it usually means that in the writing of history the writer inevitably inserts his own value system so that what is written never really corresponds to the past event. It should be pointed out, however, that few if any logical reasons for the position are given. Some illustrations are given of how different people have seen events differently, and then the position is simply stated as Toynbee does.

> Thus the historian's transcendence of self-centeredness is never more than partial and imperfect; and even contemporaries who have been brought up in different cultural milieux find it difficult to appreciate one another's mutually alien cultural heritages...[43]

It is stated that the historian selects, but that, as well as the statement that the historian cannot eliminate the personal equation, does not make it so. No number of illustrations as to how persons have been influenced by the values of their culture or of historians who have written biased history will show that this is the very nature of *all* knowledge of the past.

What then are generalizations, and to what extent are they either descriptive or interpretive statements? There are numerous types of generalizations which permit verification to varying degrees. Some are so boldly conceived that it is difficult to imagine what kind of historical data could possibly verify the statement.

> According to the way of thinking of most Indians, therefore, the essence of the individual or the particular is no more than the universal by virtue of which the individual or the particular is grounded and realized.[44]

By attributing this view to 'most Indians', verification assumes insurmountable difficulties. Historically speaking, we do not have access to the thought of 'most Indians'. And, among those that we do, would 'most' mean a simple majority, or, more likely, 'nearly all?' If the latter is the case it is a dubious statement. And, its verification would require having familiarized oneself with the thought of all or at least almost all Indians in order to be able to describe the 'way of thinking' of 'most Indians'. A statement of equal difficulty for verification is the same author's statement about the Chinese. 'The Chinese had a high regard for particulars, and presented content concretely in accordance with their way of thinking'.[45]

It might be urged that such generalizations are not meant to be infallible, but only approximations. That is apparent – but they are not a legitimate part of historical writing since they are not historically verifiable. Furthermore, familiarity with the data would also show that they are gross oversimplifications and as such correspond to nothing real. They are generalizations of descriptive intent which have a low degree of probability according to historical method.

While generalizing about all or most Indians or Chinese is difficult to verify, the following generalization is more limited and is hence more verifiable.

> The Chinese, too, under the T'ang and the Sung dynasties, produced excellent poems, but most of the ideas expressed were concrete and stayed within the natural laws of time and space.[46]

This generalization is not universal, but refers to the nature of certain (not all) poems in particular periods (T'ang and Sung). Such generalizations fall within the legitimate confines of the history of religons. But, unless the historian of religions will be content with being a dilettante, he will have to limit himself to statements which are verifiable by his method. Some of the above generalizations are not verifiable by any method with which I am familiar.

A generalization, then, is different from some types of simple historical statements, but can be either descriptive or interpretive depending on the nature of the statement. The type of evidence demanded for the verification of a generalization depends upon whether it is descriptive or interpretive and not that it is a generalization. Descriptive statements can be made that do not involve the values of the historian.[47] Generalizations can be factual statements and are then subject to the same kind of verification as statements like 'In the year 49 B. C. Caesar crossed the Rubicon.' Sometimes, moreover, generalizations can have a higher degree of probability than more simple statements regarding the date of an event for which the data are either slight or conflicting.[48]

The necessity of supplying connections
Causal statements are similar to generalizations in that they may be either descriptive or interpretive. To deal with the problems related to causation raised by Hume would be a lengthy task. The point is that historians do make statements of a causal nature, and their statements about the past seem to imply that the causal connection lies not only in the mind of the historian but

also that it was true of the past event itself. Some have denied the clear intent of their own historical statements, however, by contending that it is the mind of the historian that imposes the structure on the past.[49]

Maurice Mandelbaum points out that since Hume and Kant it has often been assumed that the structure which the objects of our knowledge possess are the results of the activity of the human mind upon a world of flux. Mandelbaum offers an opposing position: 'We hold that the order to be found in nature and history as they are known to us may really characterize the events of the world independently of the mind's activity'.[50] While not going into the matter in detail, Mandelbaum points out that if one holds that the human mind has an ordering activity, then this is to say that either the mind is not a part of nature, or that at least one element of nature, the mind, somehow has order implicit to it. If one chooses to see the mind as outside the order of nature he must accept the consequences of that statement for both his psychology and theology. Furthermore, if one holds that all structuring is due to the activity of the mind, 'why is it that the mind attributes one form of order to certain of the elements in its experience and another form of order to certain other elements'.[51] Mandelbaum explains his choice.

> On any assumption such as the Kantian this problem must remain to the end of time what Windelband calls 'a sacred mystery'. Let him who will, acknowledge such mysteries as the ultimate terminus of philosophic discussion. To us it seems preferable to start with mysteries and conclude with some definite knowledge, rather than to start from grounds of which we feel ourselves to be sure and proceed to a point where the very search for an answer becomes meaningless.[52]

Historians do make causal statements and intend to say that the causal connection indicated was in the event. The point to be made for our purposes is that causal statements may be either descriptive or interpretive and that their verification in this regard is similar to the verification of generalizations.

> We have seen that Brahmanism had hardly been formulated before vigorous dissent appeared. The Kshatriyas were particularly aroused to dissent. They did not like either the social or the religious implications of Brahmanism.[53]

The intent of this statement is causal. The writer is saying that the dissent of the Kshatriyas was caused, at least in part,[54] by their dislike of the social or religious implications of Brahmanism. This is also a descriptive statement since it can be verified by examining the appropriate textual data. The probability of this descriptive statement, then, depends upon the type of historical evidence that can be brought to its support. There is, therefore, a possible and legitimate historical answer of a descriptive nature to the 'why' of an event.

When, on the other hand, Flugel says '...this failure in the fertility of his marriage aroused superstitious fears connected with Henry's Oedipus complex', he is making a causal statement of an interpretive nature since the validity rests on two kinds of evidence. Here the question 'why' is answered not in the light of historical data, but in the light of Freudian psychology. An answer to the causal question may therefore be given at various levels, some of which are descriptive and others of which are interpretive.

Carl Becker goes further when he says that the simple fact 'In the year 49 B. C. Caesar crossed the Rubicon' has strings attached to it. This fact has significance only because of its relationship to other facts and to the interpretive structure into which it is placed.[55] If causal statements and generalizations can be either descriptive or interpretive, as we have argued, then the relationship between statements can be interpretive or descriptive as well. Becker's statement implies that descriptive or factual statements only take on meaning as they are related to other factual statements. But if such relationships are themselves descriptive (verifiable by citing historical data alone), then one must either distinguish between levels of interpretation or, better still, limit the use of the word as I have done.

It has been conceded that interpretive statements give meanings to factual or descriptive statements that they never had when they stood alone, but it has been argued that some statements which are called 'interpretive' hardly qualify for the title. The 'facts' do not exist in a vacuum, and past events were not enacted in a vacuum either. Actually, descriptive statements are based upon data from which a number of different, and sometimes related, descriptive statements can usually be made. If this is so, then the connection made between some types of descriptive statements is itself descriptive in that it is based as solidly upon the data as any single descriptive statement.

Becker reflects the mind of others as well when he says, '...generally speaking, the more simple an historical fact is, the more clear and definite and provable it is, the less use it is to us in and for itself'.[56] This statement contains a certain amount of truth. But, much depends upon what use one wants to make of the available data. It may be necessary for the discerning historian to admit that some descriptive statements cannot be used to answer certain questions no matter how interesting or profound they may be to the human spirit.

Psychological consideration

There is a very basic distinction to be made between the *psychology of history* and the *logic of history*. Morton White has pointed out this distinction in his analysis of the relativism of Charles Beard. 'Beard was guilty of a confusion which is typical in the philosophy of history, the confusion between the psychology of historical interpretation and its logic'.[57] The question is not whether the historian has interests – who doesn't? There is still the point that what stands or falls as being adequate or inadequate is the conjunction of statements that he finally writes down. This must pass the rigid criteria that historians are capable of applying. The fact that the historian of religions has certain interests is irrelevant since his interest at this point *may not be* relevant to the topic being researched, or it may be merely the neutral interest in knowing something about the past.[58] As Sidney Hook puts it:

> The possession of bias or passion on the part of the historian does not preclude the possibilty of his achieving objectivity in testing his hypothesis any more than a physician's passion to relieve men from the ravages of a disease...precludes the possiblility of a discovery of a medical... truth.[59]

The whole question of self-transcendence can be seen in the same light. When it is stated that the historian can never completely transcend his cultural and historical context, one is making a statement of a psychological nature. The question to which we want an answer is not whether one can achieve complete psychological self-transcendence. That is a meaningless question since it involves a contradiction in terms. The sentence seems to be asking whether or not man can cease to be himself. The real issue is whether the written history under consideration stands in such a way that the emotional concerns of the historian have not compromised the accuracy of the work. I know of no thinker on this subject who is proposing that one can always live in a condition of personal suspension or self-transcendence. Nor is the real issue whether one can withhold his evaluation on any subject at will. The question is whether any one person can write on any one topic in such a way that, if he has any values that are relevant to his subject, they will not intrude into his written study. I would contend that logical self-transcendence is possible if for no other reason than because it is possible to write on a subject in which one has no particular stakes except curiosity about the past. It is not only the historian who has values. The ability of the historian of religions to restrain them, and not to write on subjects for which he is emotionally disqualified may go a long way toward indicating his ability as an historian of religions. If one is too involved to even recognize his involvement, then we simply cannot expect an objective account from him. But, it does not follow that since some or even many written histories fit this category, that therefore all of them do. By operating under functional definitions and by limiting history to an accurate description of the human past, we could assist ourselves in the direction of accuracy since we have disavowed the possibility of settling theological questions in this manner.

Relativism and probability

Having argued for the possibility of objectivity, we have repeatedly asserted that statements in history can only be highly probable at best. One of the problems in the discussion of this issue is the confusion of historical relativism with historical probability. The opposite of relativism is objectivity, and the opposite of absolutism is probability. We have argued against relativism since it seems to forfeit the possibility of knowing anything. This is not to argue that any work of history can be absolute (either in the sense of total knowledge or in the sense of absolute certainty).

It might be argued that in our position the validity of the statement is relative to the evidence available to support it. It is also relative to the question asked. But this is not what is commonly intended by the use of the word relative and is not what we have been rejecting. Historical relativity proposes that the statement is relative to the *viewer* regardless of what kind of evidence one marshals to its support. It has been our point that the validity of the statement does not depend upon understanding how or why it was stated by the person who stated it, but whether and to what extent the data bears it up. This can be analyzed without concern for Mannheim's 'sociology of knowledge'. To say that the probability of a statement is relative to the evidence would be a truism to which any staunch objectivist would submit. But it is not saying anything more than that the probability of a statement depends on the amount and kind of evidence that can be used to defend it. It is quite another thing when one says that no matter what the evidence, the statement is less than adequate, not because of a lack of evidence, but because it happens to be a culture-bound man who makes the statement.

It is necessary to grant that no historical statement can be more than highly probable. But to say this is to admit the possibility of objective statements about the past. If all statements or written histories are relative to the viewer, then from the standpoint of testing them, none are more probable than others. The concept of probability makes sense only as one concedes that objectivity is possible, and I would suggest, this is implied when a historian makes a judgment that this written history is more true to the data than is another one. Given the logic of the relativist approach, one is hard pressed to object to any written history.

Functional definitions and historical knowledge

How does our use of functional definitions and our choice of meanings for the words to be defined relate to this question of the possibility of historical knowledge? In particular, it indicates clearly the limits of applicability of the statements that an historian of religions makes. Such definitions indicate that when the historian of religions is talking about religion, he is talking about ultimate concern; when he is talking about history he is talking about a descriptive knowledge of the human past. By using functional definitions, one is avoiding the theological question that Kraemer thinks is inevitable.

There is little doubt that the very choice of meanings for these words reflects certain values. In addition to indicating the logical limits of an inquiry, such definitions probably indicate that the scholar thinks such questions are worth asking. This must be conceded. I will go a step further. Although the descriptive study of the human past can never answer ultimate questions on the normative level, the religious question is probably the most significant *historical* question that one can ask. One would be hard pressed to hold that it is not of high importance to ascertain what has been most important to men individually and in community. But admitting that the question reflects the values of the researcher is simply to admit that for another people and another age the study of religion might be (and indeed it has been) other than the study of ultimate concern. This is the nature of functional definitions which are semi-arbitrary. But that admission does not relativize the religio-historical answer derived from an examination of the data. It merely indicates the answer is relative *to the question*. That should be obvious. And, it is no threat to a valid knowledge of man's religious past. The use of functional definitions in this manner will not guarantee religio-historical knowledge. That will always depend in part on the ability and resolve of historians of religions.

4

The Category of Understanding

Methodology stands out as the single most important problem for the history of religions. Let us be frank about it. There is no lack of material for our speculations. The researchers in the various linguistic and other humanistic disciplines have recorded an enormous amount of relevant data which aside from whatever other uses they may have, apply to the work of the historico-religious interpreter as well. Without an adequate method for handling these materials, our uses of them become mere improvisions.[1]

White's emphasis on methodology, and the emphasis placed on this by other historians of religions is not without purpose. As they see it, an adequate methodology is required if we are to 'understand' the religions of other men. For this reason White's essay begins with a section on 'The Problem of Understanding'.

Surely the historian of religions does not wish less than to understand the whole religion of which he studies only parts (or the whole of the religious of which the religions are only parts).[2]

Not only has the word 'understanding' found its way into the subtitle of this entire volume of essays, but it occurs repeatedly in the content of several of the essays. Kitagawa's 'Primitive, Classical, and Modern Religions: A Perspective on Understanding the History of Religions', begins, as does White's essay, with a section on 'Problem of Understanding'. Perhaps it is not inappropriate, then, that the lead essay for the volume is by Joachim Wach, whose three-volume *Das Verstehen* is well-known.[3] In Wach's contribution, 'The Meaning and Task of the History of Religions' the central concern of the history of religions is defined in terms of its ability to 'understand'.

From what has been discussed, it should be clear that the central concern of *Religionswissenschaft* must be the understanding of other religions.[4]

The problem of 'understanding', then, has frequently been a central methodological consideration in the history of religions.When 'understanding' is not explicitly named, it frequently lurks behind methodological discussions. The amount of space given to methodological considerations by historians of religions reflects their desire to develop a method which will enable them to 'understand' the religions of others.

Occasionally this concern for 'understanding' goes even further, and then one is left with the impression that it is the goal of 'understanding' which distinguishes the history of religions from theology, sociology, anthropology, psychology, and other related disciplines. Sometimes this is even stated explicitly.

> Furthermore, it must be kept in mind that the historian of religions is engaged in the religio-scientific inquiry of religions for the sake of 'understanding', and not for the service of the propagation of any particular faith. While we recognize the important role of a 'theological history of religions', this is a theological discipline, and we must maintain a wholesome tension between the history of religions and a theological history of religions.[5]

But the goal of 'understanding' is seen to be a difficult one, and the question is commonly raised as to whether it is even possible to 'understand' religions other than one's own. In his essay 'On Understanding Non-Christian Religions', Ernst Benz enumerates certain problems he encountered in seeking to understand Far Eastern religions, even after he had read a great deal about them.[6]

Some of these difficulties are the following:

1. The difficulty of translating from one language to another when there is no equivalent for key words.
2. Similar historical, philosophical, and theological assumptions are missing both in the intellectual, and more important, in the emotional dimension.
3. Christian and Western presuppositions which we hold, sometimes unconsciously.
    a) The personalistic idea of God.
    b) The preference for monotheism over polytheism.
    c) Essential distinction between Creator and creation.
4. The common preference for theology among Christians while in the East more is made of ritualistic and artistic modes of expression.

5. The lack of a parallel with Western means of religious organization.
6. The ease with which many Easterners are 'members' of more than one so called 'religion'.
7. The prevalence of magic and sorcery in other religious traditions.
8. The difficulty in understanding the practice of sacrifice and its meaning.
9. The basis of mission in other religious traditions.

Benz does not see these as insurmountable, but merely as difficulties which he encountered in his effort to 'understand'. Other historians of religions might encounter different difficulties.

It is seldom held that such problems are insuperable. If it were to be admitted that 'understanding' other religions were not possible, the historian of religions would have nothing further to do. Sometimes it is held that only someone who is a member of a religious group or community is capable of understanding the religion of that group. But Wach's analysis of membership refutes such a claim.[7] Membership is often determined by birth, particularly in tribal cultures. Then, there are 'members' who know less about the intended meaning of certain rites in which they participate than do intelligent observers. As Wach puts it,

> Could it seriously be maintained that a great scholar belonging to Group A would be less capable of understanding the religion of Group B than any ignorant and humble person belonging to the latter? Obviously official membership cannot be the criterion for the possibility of understanding.[8]

To this one must add two other points. The *first* is that it is commonly the experience of fieldworkers that different participants in the same rite offer different explanations of the meaning of the rite. This phenomenon suggests that there is no single 'meaning' to be given ritual or cult practice. Milton Singer points out that 'many different kinds of people participate in these performances for many different kinds of individual reasons'.[9] The *second* is the fact of conversion. There are occasionally persons who leave one religious community for another by reason of conversion. It is the confession of such persons that they have been presented with something new and have accepted it. To deny that one can understand a religion other than one's own would be to deny the witness of conversion experiences.

'Understanding' is often conceived in such a way that it is more than a mere knowledge of the facts.[10] This is why it is often related to hermeneutics, for understanding involves 'interpretation' or 'integration'.

'To understand' requires examination of specific, concrete data – data such as ideas in literature and descriptions of rituals, social institutions, historical developments, lives of great personalities, and political and social conditions. But it does not mean the mere stockpiling of unrelated facts. 'To understand' means that one is aware of a principle of selectivity that serves as a filter for interpretation. 'To understand' means to integrate data according to a context of interpretation – a context that does not give every element in an experience equal weight, but rather provides the categories and concerns that permit one to relate the data in a certain way.[11]

Because of the integrative function of 'understanding', empathy with the believers studied is frequently a stated requirement. But empathy stops short of belief. If the historian of religions is ever to reach the goal of 'understanding' other religions, belief must not be a desideratum. Otherwise one could only understand as many forms of religion as he could simultaneously believe. One need hardly spell out the implications of such a ludicrous situation. But sympathy or empathy is important.

But there is a difference between 'understanding' and 'believing', and it is not true that we cannot understand another religious form unless we personally believe it, and thus 'enter' it. 'To understand' means to appreciate how it is possible for a person to believe what he does, given the presuppositions that he holds; 'to believe' means to accept the presuppositions about life and to live according to them.[12]

The goal of understanding is felt most critically when it aims at the innermost experiences of men. Even within religious traditions there is recognized what Wach has called the principle of irreversability. By this principle it is recognized that one who has achieved a higher degree of realization or insight can perceive what is going on in the person who has achieved a lower level of experience. But the reverse is not the case. Hence an enlightened Zen Roshi can distinguish authentic Zen art (done by an enlightened master) from apparently identical copies (done by sympathetic but unenlightened artists), even though persons who have not achieved *satori* are not equally discriminative. And, since this irreversability is self-authenticating, it cannot be questioned or doubted.

It follows, then, that part of the answer to the question of whether we can understand religions other than our own depends on the depths of understanding which one desires. Ultimately, there are depths which one can hardly hope to understand within oneself. As one probes toward the inner concentric circles of human experience, understanding becomes less possible than it was with the more accessible outer circles. Hence the difficulty of answering Benz's question: 'What moves the devout Hindu to pass by the Kali temple and the Vishnu temple on one day, and hurry to the sanctuary of Krishna to offer him his sacrifice of flowers and his prayers and to participate the next day in the Kali festival?'

The historian of religions must recognize that there are depths which he cannot investigate. Other methods *might* investigate such depths. But, unless we want to suppose that a *complete* understanding is possible for finite men, we will have to concede that there are depths of reality which are beyond human investigation. This does not mean that such depths are clearly distinguishable. It may be *heuristically* feasible to hold that everything is investigatable. But as we probe into the more private depths of human experience (i.e. those areas not part of universal human experience), verification becomes less possible, and understanding correspondingly less likely. As one moves more into such interior realms, one must construct statements which have increasingly lower levels of probability. And, statements that are only slightly probable, or merely possible, however interesting they might be were they highly probable, are hardly worth a high priority among scholars.

The possibility of understanding is determined not only by the depths of human experience one is attempting to 'understand', but also the level on which one's attempt takes place. The two questions are not unrelated, for the level or method of investigation must be appropriate to the object (or subject) being investigated. Our methods may be unable to probe certain depths of experience.

It comes as little surprise to find that the word 'understanding' is ambiguous. We have found that this was true for 'religion' and 'history'. Most words that have common usage are ambiguous in that they are used in several conflicting ways. Hence, 'understanding' must be clarified with a functional definition.

In chapter three, a distinction was made between the psychology and the logic of history. Here it is necessary to make a distinction between the psychology and the logic of understanding. The former points to the interior apprehension of the historian of religions and the latter to the available results of his research. Sometimes 'understanding' is so internalized that it is contrasted with merely 'knowing the facts'.[13] I would like to reverse this emphasis by offering as a functional definition of 'understanding' religion any valid knowledge about religion communicable in propositional form. This is not to deny that knowledge *about* religion is not the same as knowledge *of* religion in an existential and experiential sense. Nor does it deny the possibility of the latter. What is denied is that religious experience is a valid goal for the historian of religions as an academician. Academic study and research is admittedly penultimate. But such an admission should assist us in avoiding religious experience as an operative part of the methodology of the historian of religions.

If understanding may be assumed to have taken place when valid knowledge about a religion has been communicated in propositional form, this places the point to be verified in what we say about the religions of men and not in the psychological dimension of emotional empathy which we did or did not possess during the investigation. Such empathy may well be a psychological requirement for the achievement of understanding as here defined, but it becomes clear that it is our *statements* that are on trial and not the degree of empathy which is necessarily difficult if not impossible to verify. The statements are verifiable or falsifiable in a way that empathy is not.

Furthermore, if an 'understanding' of religion is achieved when valid knowledge about religion has been acquired, then it follows that the history or religions is not to be distinguished from other disciplines in its goal of 'understanding'. Such would mean that other disciplines have no valid knowledge. And, apart from the concern such a position might raise among theologians and anthropologists (to mention only two groups), it simply is not true.

There are no strictly religious data. There are human data, of which a variety of questions may be asked. To the extent that the answers to these questions are probable and valid, to that extent understanding has taken place. While certain types of religion may be mystical, *the study* of religion has no reason to be so.

I would like, in this chapter, to examine several levels of understanding and to indicate the limits within which they operate. My position has been that religio-historical understanding has occurred when descriptively true statements about a given person or group can be constructed which indicate what is ultimately important to that person or group. This has been fully articulated in chapters two and three. But it is necessary to conceed that this is not the only question that can be asked of the human data. Nor has it been the only question that has been asked in the name of 'religion'. Hence, we will proceed to examine several other levels of 'understanding'.

Some of these levels are not in conflict with religio-historical study as defined in this volume: they might enrich certain dimensions of such study. Others, however, while perhaps legitimate in their own right, add little to religio-historical study. This much must be said: since these are different levels of investigation and understanding, and since they issue in different levels of knowledge, they are not always questions which can be asked simultaneously. We will see that it is not possible to ask the historical and the phenomenological questions simultaneously. The same can be said for the historical and the normative. Occasionally the functional question and the religio-historical question are identical while on other occasions they are not. The determination of personal faith may often be identical with the religious question. Hence the method of Wilfred Cantwell Smith is most helpful.

We will center our discussion in each case around a given thinker (or thinkers). While such an approach cannot pretend to be exhaustive, it can be useful. We will see that the method and content of understanding is different on each of these levels. For Malinowski, one has understood a religious rite when he has determined its psychological or social function. For Wilfred Cantwell Smith one has understood the faith of another when that 'other' is able to affirm our construction of it. For Mircea Eliade, one has understood a rite, myth, or symbol when he has seen it in the perspective of universal structures. For Radhakrishnan one has understood a religion when he sees it as a manifestation of *Sanātana Dharma*. For both the normative and the phenomenological levels, understanding does not involve the recognition of authenticity on the part of the believer.

A. FUNCTIONAL UNDERSTANDING: BRONISLAW MALINOWSKI

There are numerous variations to functional theory, and the literature is voluminous. Functional analysis has been applied to psychology, political science, economics, sociology, geography, jurisprudence, and linguistics.

However, 'it is probably true that of all the social sciences it is anthropology which has made fullest capital of the functionalist approach'.[14]

While on the one hand functionalism has been subjected to certain telling criticisms,[15] on the other hand it has been denied that functionalism is a distinct mode of sociological analysis.[16] Such debates may be important for anthropologists, but they do not presently concern us. We are more interested in the logic of the functional understanding of religion, and what it might mean to understand a rite, belief, or other religious expression on the level of functional understanding.

Robert K. Merton has pointed out what he calls 'prevailing postulates in functional analysis'.[17] There are three such postulates, and each is espoused by Malinowski. The first postulate of much functional analysis is the functional unity of society. Perhaps Malinowski unduly universalized his experience with the Tobriand Islanders, but he held that society was a unit. He listed as two of several general axioms of functionalism that culture is a 'system of objects, activities, and attitudes in which every part exists as a means to an end' and that culture is an 'integral in which the various elements are interdependent'.[18] Each item in the society has a function in relationship to the society *as a whole*. This is particularly true when one considers the function of the supernatural, an important part of a working definition of religion for not a few anthropologists.

> Here the functional view is put to its acid test. What can be the function of primitive belief and superstition, or animism considered as valueless, crude and mistaken, or magic, regarded as a spurious and falacious psuedo-science, or totemism, of barbarious burial ceremonies and of cruel initiation rites? And yet the method here set forth stands and falls with the possibility of defining the whole of the supernatural. It is bound to show in what way belief and ritual work for social integration, technical and economic efficiency, *for culture as a whole* – indirectly therefore for the biological and mental welfare *of each individual member*.[19]

This statement includes the basis for the contention that functionalism is ideologically conservative and that for Malinowski religion is always productive of social integration.

The second postulate is the closely related notion of universal functionalism. It holds that *all* standardized cultural forms have positive functions. The functional view insists therefore upon the principle that in every type of civilization. every custom, material object, idea and belief fulfills some vital function, has some task to accomplish, represents an indispensable part within a working whole.[20]

For Malinowski, society is analogous to biological organisms in that *each part* functions toward the well-being of the whole. It is this which made it difficult for Malinowski to conceive of religion as having dysfunctional as well as functional social roles. The evolutionary view had posited non-functional cultural survivals from previous stages in the evolutionary process. Malinowski held that *all items* had a function, and that the evolutionary view could be used to support such a position

Again since the essence of evolution consists not in a sequence of different forms changing one into another, but in a better adaptation of an institution to its function, the more precise way of posing the evolutionary problem leads inevitably to the functional point of view.[21]

The postulate of universal functionalism is explained historically by Merton as the result of the controversy in anthropological ranks over 'survivals'. Social survivals were social customs which supposedly could not be explained in terms of their social function but only in terms of their past history.

In consequence, perhaps, they over-reacted against this concept central to evolutionary theory and advanced an equally exaggerated 'postulate' to the effect that 'every custom (everywhere) ...fulfills some vital function'.[22]

The third postulate is functional indispensability. Malinowski holds that each item in culture, whether material object or belief 'fulfills some vital function'.[23] Such a point of view later led to the view of 'functional prerequisites', or conditions which are fundamentally necessary for society to exist. We will examine whether such postulates are necessary to functional understanding. But now we turn to the way in which these principles form a basis for Malinowski's analysis of religion in social perspective.

Magic and religion

Sir James Frazer held that magic was the sister of science, because he saw it working according to laws. These laws are known to the magician. But magic is an infant science since it does not fully understand the laws it attempts to utilize. Magic does not involve requests to superhuman beings. If the magic is properly performed, the result is certain. By contrast, religion affirms the existence and power of superhuman beings who can change the course of natural events. Hence it is fundamentally different from magic which assumes unchanging mechanical laws. Religion grew out of the inadequacy of magic. When magicians were unable to control the world, then, it was assumed, there must be mightier beings who can. Religion results from the realization that magic does not suffice, and originates only when responsible people gain this insight and reflect on the consequences.

Malinowski rejects Frazer's view. To begin with, the pre-literate does distinguish between a type of scientific knowledge and magical practices. Magic is never relied upon to bear the total load of success. In the preparation of boats, fishing methods, and warfare, the preliterate is aware of the various precautions that must be part of one's calculations. But after all the available knowledge has been utilized, there is still the possibility of failure due to unpredictable occurrences such as storm at sea. Hence magic has the function of enabling man to cope with the unexpected and that which he cannot foresee.

The role of magic is illustrated by the fishing practices of the Tobriand Islanders.

> While in the villages on the inner lagoon fishing is done in an easy and absolutely reliable manner by the method of poisoning, yielding abundant results without danger and uncertainty, there are on the shores of the open sea dangerous modes of fishing and also certain types in which the yield greatly varies according to whether shoals of fish appear beforehand or not. It is most significant that in the lagoon fishing, where man can rely completely upon his knowledge and skill, magic does not exist, while in the open-sea fishing, full of danger and uncertainty, there is extensive magical ritual to secure safety and with good results.[24]

The pre-literate never relies on magic alone although he sometimes eliminates it completely. Nevertheless, magic and science are quite different. Pre-literate man does engage in a type of practical 'science'.

> The native shipwright knows not only practically of buoyancy, leverage, equilibrium, he has to obey these laws not only in water, but while making the canoe he must have the principles in his mind. He instructs his helpers in them. He gives them the traditional rules, and in a crude and simple manner, using his hands, pieces of wood, and a limited technical vocubulary, he explains some general laws of hydrodynamics and equilibrium.[25]

Magic is never used to replace work. The pre-literate knows that gardens do not grow on magic alone, but that digging and the clearing of the ground is required if one is to have a successful harvest. And so, in terms of Frazer's view that magic is primitive science, Malinowski concludes:

> Magic therefore far from being primitive science, is the outgrowth of clear recognition that science has its limits and that a human mind and human skill are at times impotent.[26]

Magic has a function not only in enabling men to cope with the unexpected: it also serves as an organizing force in society. Because the magician has a special knowledge, and controls the practical activities associated with magical rites, he is a person of great significance in the community. Magic serves as a real organizing force for society because of the public aspect of the magical rites.

While religion also has its function for the individual and for society, there is a basic difference between it and magic.

> For magic is distinguished from religion in that the latter creates values and attains ends directly, whereas magic consists of acts which have a practical utilitarian value and are effective only as a means to an end.[27]

In the typically religious act the end is realized in the consummation of the act itself. Religion is a way of satisfying man's psychological, social, and biological needs.[28] Religion is not merely speculation, but is born from the tragic element of human existence which is best seen as the conflict between human plans and realities.

Even though Malinowski interprets religion in terms of its function, he is not led to devalue it on that account. On the contrary, since it provides a cohesion for society, religion is to be valued. Every important crisis of human life implies a strong emotional upheaval with the possibility of disintegration. Religion enables man to get through such crises positively.

> Religious belief consists in the traditional standardization of the positive side in the mental conflict and therefore satisfies a definite individual need arising out of the psychological concomitants of social organization. On the other hand, religious belief and ritual, by making the critical acts and the social contracts of human life public, traditionally standardized, and subject to supernatural sanctions, strengthen the bonds of human cohesion.[29]

Religion thereby becomes one of the most powerful forces for social control. The transcendent reference (which is the testimony of religious experience) is not of primary consideration here. It figures into the analysis at the point at which it has a social function. Hence, the functional analysis of religion is in reality more of an analysis of society than it is an analysis of religion.

Religion and initiatory rites

Rites of initiation, common in pre-literate cultures, are often brutal. The novice may be taken outside of society for an extended period of time during which preparation is made. In the initiation itself there are a series of ordeals in which incisions might be made, tongues cut until blood flows profusely, teeth knocked out, or circumcision inflicted. This latter must be considered quite painful when it is remembered that the 'operation' takes place at puberty without the deadening of the senses and with a 'knife' that is often less than sharp. Malinowski sees three things that are part of the rite of initiation. The *first* is the ordeal. The *second* is the systematic instruction of the youth in the sacred lore of the tradition and the learning of the tribal mysteries. The *third* feature is that the first two elements are usually held to have been instituted by deities and hence one is imitating the deities in this rite.

In evaluating the significance of the rites of initiation, Malinowski places emphasis on the second feature – the function that the rites have in transmitting the traditional culture.

> Now what is the sociological function of these customs, what part do they play in the maintenance and development of civilization? As we have seen, the youth is taught in them the sacred traditions under the most impressive conditions of preparation and ordeal and under the sanction of Supernatural Beings – the light of tribal revelation bursts upon him from out of the shadow of fear, privation, and bodily pain.[30]

Here the main point is the preservation of the tradition. The significance of the ordeal and the calling in of the supernatural sanction merely lends force to the continuing tradition. The real point of the ritual is the preservation of the tradition, and the ordeal and the deities make this preservation a weighty and significant matter.

We are reminded by Malinowski of the conservative elements in primitive societies and the emphasis placed upon conformity. Social order can only be maintained as long as members conform to traditional knowledge. To depart from tradition threatens social cohesion and hence the very existence of society. Malinowski summarizes the function of initiation ceremonies as follows:

> We may, therefore, lay down the main function of initiation ceremonies: they are a ritual and dramatic expression of the supreme power and value of tradition in primitive societies; they also serve to impress this power and value upon the minds of each generation, and they are at the same time an extremely efficient means of transmitting tribal lore, or insuring continuity in tradition and of maintaining tribal cohesion.[31]

While the rites have their social function, they are nevertheless religious as well in that the ceremony is not intended to be a means to an end, but is one with its purpose. The end is realized in the consummation of the act. In this transitional rite, manhood with all its duties, privileges, and responsibilities is realized.

Religion and marriage

Marriage is necessary in society in that it provides an orderly means for the procreation and the rearing of children. The family is also an economic unit which enables a man and woman to live together in a life-long partnership of affection. Marriage is primarily a biological fact. But religions 'create a supernaturally sanctioned bond'.[32] When marriage is considered sacred or religious the significance of this for Malinowski is that it gives to marriage the sanction of the deities.

Religion and death

As death approaches, the family, and sometimes the entire community, is summoned. Hence death, which is in some respects the most private event in the human continuum, is made a public event. Close relatives perform rites and onlookers are permitted to come within varying distances of the body. When death occurs, the body is washed and adorned. For Malinowski the important phase of the proceedings is the mourning. Among primitives this emotional outburst sometimes passes into bodily lacerations and tearing out of the hair. Significant is the ambivalence implied in this activity and the fact that it is done in public. The corpse is the center of attention.

Often there are ritual forms of fondling or attestations of reverence. The body is sometimes kept on the knees of seated persons, stroked or embraced. At the same time these acts are usually considered both dangerous and repugnant, duties to be fulfilled at some cost to the performer. After a time the corpse has to be disposed of. Inhumation with an open or closed grave; exposure in caves or on platforms, in hollow trees or on the ground in some wild desert place; burning or setting adrift in canoes – these are the usual forms of disposal.[33]

Of considerable importance is the ambivalence of such proceedings and the possible threat to social cohesion. Malinowski detects in such proceedings the desire to preserve the body and keep it intact. This is sometimes seen in the desire to retain some part or parts of the body. On the other hand, the apparently opposite desire also appears to be present – the desire to get rid of the body and annihilate it completely. He sees mumification and cremation as the two extreme forms of this ambivalence. Each of these two cases is an example of one or the other tendency to win out. There is the longing to retain the dead person while at the same time one experiences disgust in the presence of the dead body. Malinowski regards sacro-cannibalism as a case in point. Although the flesh of the corpse is consumed, it is followed by a violent fit of vomiting.

Death is a threat to the cohesion of society. The death of a person in primitive society, particularly in the case of individuals of significant standing, is profoundly serious. Since the community is often comparatively small and closely knit, it is left in a mutilated state. Death is so shocking to the community that it could possibly pose a threat to the solidarity of the group itself. The social structure is in jeopardy.

The strong tendency on which we have insisted in the above description: to give way to fear and horror, to abandon the corpse, to run away from the village, to destroy all the belongings of the dead one – all these impulses exist, and if given way to would be extremely dangerous, disintegrating the group, destroying the material foundations of primitive culture. Death in a primitive society is, therefore, much more than the removal of a member. By setting in motion one part of the deep forces of the instinct of self-preservation, it threatens the very cohesion and solidarity of the group, and upon this depends the organization of that society, its tradition, and finally the whole culture. For if primitive man yielded always to the disintegrating impulses of his reaction to death, the continuity of tradition and the existence of material civilization would be made impossible.[34]

At this time religion offers its supreme gift: the belief in immortality. Here
religion assists man in choosing the affirmative rather than the destructive side
of the ambivalence.

> And here into this play of emotional forces, into this supreme dilemma of
> life and final death, religion steps in, selecting the positive creed, the
> comforting view, the culturally valuable belief in immortality, in the
> spirit independent of the body, and in the continuance of life after death.
> In the various ceremonies at death, in commemoration and communion
> with the departed, and worship of ancestral ghosts, religion gives body
> and form to the saving beliefs.[35]

This is a religious ceremony. The intention of the act is achieved in its per-
formance. The proceedings do not function to take the dead smoothly to
an other world, but in terms of Malinowski's method, they function in solid-
ifying the group against possible disintegration due to the loss of a member.
The mourning and rituals express the emotion of the whole group. They
enable the living to participate in the funeral rituals and thus prepare them for
their own death. Since the ceremonies are done in a group, the group is
solidified against being dissolved. Of such ceremonies Malinowski states:

> They endorse and duplicate the natural feelings of the survivors; they
> create a social event out of a natural fact. Yet, though in the acts of
> mourning, in the mimic despair of wailing, in the treatment of the corpse
> and in its disposal, nothing ulterior is achieved, these acts fulfill an
> important function and possess a considerable value for primitive
> culture.[36]

Religion and totemism

For Malinowski, totemism is another social phenomenon with religious
sanction. Primitive societies are often gravely concerned with the question
of the abundance of food. Certain animals and vegetables which form the
staple food of a given tribe dominate their interests, That animal which is
habitually pursued 'forms a nucleus round which all the interests, the impulses, the emotions of a tribe tend to crystalize'.[37] In addition to the concern
to provide an abundance of food, primitives delight in certain animals much
as do small children.

> By their general affinity with man – they move, utter sounds, manifest
> emotions, have bodies and faces like him – and by their superior powers –

the birds fly in the open, the fishes swim under water, reptiles renew their skins and their life and can disappear in the earth – by all this the animal, the intermediate link between man and nature, often his superior in strength, agility, and cunning, usually his indispensable quarry, assumes an exceptional place in the savage's view of the world.[38]

These interests converge so that primitive man makes a selection. The selection of a totemic animal from which the tribe is supposed to have come enables man to control the species. He has affinity with it but also power over it. Certain regulations prohibit the killing and eating of the totemic animal, although sacramental meals are permitted at specific times. In this way the totemic structure and regulations enable the tribe to protect the species and thus assure their abundance.

From the survival point of view, it is vital that man's interest in the practically indispensable species should never abate, that his belief in his capacity to control them should give him strength and endurance in his pursuits and stimulate his observations and knowledge of the habits and natures of animals and plants. Totemism appears thus as a blessing best wed by religion on primitive man's efforts in dealing with his useful surroundings, upon his 'struggle for existence'.[39]

Totemism is the religion of the clan, and impresses upon the members the totemic taboo and a reverential attitude toward the species. It issues in public ceremonies which help to impress the taboos upon the tribal members – thereby strengthening social solidarity.

Religion and myth

Malinowski approaches myth much as he approaches rites and beliefs. He is not interested in the theological symbolism involved even though he recognizes that it is closely connected with religion and with ritual. He rejects the view of the school of Nature-mythology which sees mythology as an attempt to express and interpret the forces of nature such as the sun, the wind, or the phases of the moon.

Some of these departmental mythologists fight fiercely for their heavenly body or principle; others have a more catholic taste, and prepare to agree that primeval man has made his mythological brew from all the heavenly bodies taken together.[40]

In addition to seeing primitive man as concerned about something that he is not, this interpretation ignores the cultural function of myth. Theories as to whether myth is the sacred history of the tribe, the celestial reasonings of the tribe, or the daydream of the race, are of little interest to Malinowski. What he wants to know is what function myth plays in society. It is for this reason that he chides those who rely on texts and never study primitive society on the spot. Some levels of understanding do not require on-the-spot observation. But if one is interested in the function the myth plays in society, fieldwork appears necessary. Social function often cannot be read from the text: it must be observed in the actions and rites of the people themselves.

Myth is not an idle tale, but a significant force in society. It has a very practical function.

Myth fulfills in primitive culture an indispensable function: it expresses, enhances, and codifies belief; it safeguards and enforces morality; it vouches for the efficiency of ritual and contains practical rules for the guidance of man.[41]

Malinowski distinguishes between three types of tales in use among the Tobriand Islanders. There is the *kukwanebu* which is told at certain seasons by people who 'own' them. The *kukwanebu* are mainly for entertainment. There is the *libwogwo* which may be historical accounts, legends, or hearsay tales which are believed to be true and which open past historical vistas. The *myth* 'comes to play when rite, ceremony, or a social or moral rule demands justification, warrant of antiquity, reality, and sanctity'.[42] Myth is not intended to add information but to offer a warrant and perhaps give a practical guide to the rituals with which it is connected. The important thing about the myth is its function, which is to strengthen tradition, 'and endow it with a greater value and prestige by tracing it back to a higher, better, more supernatural reality of initial events'.[43]

It is emphatically denied that the myth is an attempt of the primitive to explain something. Nor is myth to be thought of as 'primitive science'.

Nothing is more familiar to the native man than the different occupations of the male and female sex; there is nothing to be *explained* about it. But though familiar, such differences are at times irksome, unpleasant, or at least limiting, and there is the need to justify them, to vouch for their antiquity and reality, in short to buttress their validity.[44]

A Melanesian myth of origin describes the world as originally being peopled from underground. People originally emerged from the underground with fixed villages, clans, districts, and with distinctions of rank and responsibility. Functional analysis understands this mythological account in its detail (including a dialogue between a dog and a pig) in terms of its ability to determine social roles and responsibilities. Living among the people, one ascertains that the myth is in constant use in settling disagreements over the relative superiority of the various clans.

Once you know the native sociology, the extreme importance of rank, the fact that food and its limitations (the taboos of rank and clan) are the main index of man's social nature, and finally the psychology of totemic identification – you begin to understand how this incident, happening as it did when humanity was *in statu nascendi*, settled once for all the relation between the two rival clans. To understand this myth you must have a good knowledge of their sociology, religion, customs, and outlook. Then, and only then, can you appreciate what this story means to the natives and how it can live in their life.[45]

Limits of functional understanding

There is no need to retreat from functional understanding on the grounds that it is reductionistic. Indeed, it can be reductionist, as can any level of investigation, when it assumes that it exhausts the meaning of the given data. Some of Malinowski's statements open him to such criticism. Any method implies its own limitations of meaning, and if Malinowski's more extreme statements are taken within the limits of applicability of social function, they can be formally acceptable. In at least one place Malinowski explicitly makes room for other levels of investigation. When speaking of the instinct of self-preservation and the common occurrence of the notion of immorality, he says:

Whether this is achieved by a Providence directly guiding human history, or by a process of natural selection in which a culture which evolves a belief and a ritual of immortality will survive and spread – this is a problem of theology or metaphysics.[46]

Furthermore, one need not subscribe to Malinowski's theory that culture functions basically to supply man's biological needs in order to grant the usefulness of functional understanding. And, if by satisfactory explanation one means one 'that says more than a circular explanation, that is, the *explicans* contains statements which go beyond what is to be explained',[47] it can be conceeded that functional analysis does not provide a valid explanation.

Explanations are satisfactory when they indicate why a thing happens rather than does not happen, and why *that thing* happens rather than something else. Ultimately, explanations that are valid should lead to social laws.

It is even possible, as Merton has cogently shown, to maintain the values of functional analysis without sharing the three prevailing postulates which Malinowski accepted. As for the first, the functional unity of society, Merton observes:

> Whether cultural items do uniformly fulfill functions for the society viewed as a system and for all members of the society is presumably an empirical question of fact, rather than an axiom.[48]

Furthermore, the empirical evidence in the case of religion seems to indicate that when different religious systems exist in the same society there often occurs inter-religious conflict. Religion, therefore, does not always function for the integration of society as a whole.

The second postulate of universal functionalism is also a 'problem for investigation, not a conclusion in advance of investigation'.[49] And, as for the postulate of functional indispensability, it fails to recognize the possibility of functional alternatives. It cannot be held prior to the investigation of empirical evidence that religion is even an indispensable prerequisite for a stable society, for that would be to assume that religion is the only alternative for control over human conduct. Merton puts it succinctly.

> *...just as the same item may have multiple functions, so may the same function be diversely fulfilled by alternative items.* Functional needs are here taken to be permissive, rather than determinant, of specific social structures. Or, in other words, there is a range of variation in the structures which fulfill the function in question.[50]

Once the metaphysical aspect of the 'prevalent postulates of functionalism' are deleted, it is possible to utilize functional understanding heuristically. Perhaps Malinowski was finally coming to such a position when he said: 'Thus I suggest the concept of function with reference to certain wide, separate institutional groups, primarily as a heuristic device.'[51] The notion of the functional unity of society or the seamlessness of society is actually non-falsifiable for it *cannot* clash with empirical evidence. If it appears to do so, one can only conclude that the social unity has simply not yet been found, or the function of a given item is not yet known. This should indicate the metaphysical or ontological dimension of such postulates when taken universally.

Taken heuristically, however, functional understanding has provided some interesting insights into the use of religion. The question which the functional question actually attempts to answer is one of the broader connections and relationships. As I. C. Jarvie puts it: 'Some actions and institutions have nonobvious connections with others. Do not forget to look for these.'[52] Even though one might wish to give up the postulate of universal functionalism, the wholistic view of society, and the postulate of functional indispensability, it remains useful to observe the functions which certain items have in society even if they function differently in subgroups within the same society. Functionalism as a heuristic device may have to admit that it cannot find a function for some item. But that does not matter either. One is looking for functions *when* they occur, and *when* they can be found. This fits in well with Merton's definition of functionalism:

> The central orientation of functionalism – expressed in the practice of interpreting data by establishing their consequences for larger structures in which they are implicated...[53]

In such a manner functional analysis escapes the judgment that it is either ideologically conservative or ideologically radical.[54] Functional analysis conceived as a heuristic device is ideologically neutral. It is the values that one places upon what is found through functional analysis that are either 'conservative' or 'radical'.

Finally, on the functional level of understanding, the witness of the believer is useful, but it is not necessarily a check on accuracy as it will be for the personalist approach. Not infrequently the reported motives of participants are confused with the goal of functional analysis. It may be a useful part of functional analysis to include an account of the motivations of the participants in a given religious rite. Some may even assist in determing the psychological function of the rite in the case of given individuals. But that should not be confused with the objective pattern of behavior. To speak of the function of a social item is not the same as to speak of its 'purpose' or the 'motives' people have in performing it. Functional analysis is concerned with the *objective social consequences* of a belief or rite which is not infrequently something quite different from what was intended by the participant. Merton introduced the concepts of manifest and latent functions to account for this distinction. For Merton, manifest functions 'are those objective consequences contributing to the adjustment or adaptation of the system which are intended and recognized by participants in the system'.[55] Latent functions are 'those which are neither intended nor recognized'.[56] In other words, there may be objective consequences of religion which are either anticipated or unanticipated, and these may be either functional or dysfunctional.

B. PHENOMENOLOGICAL UNDERSTANDING: MIRCEA ELIADE

If the functional understanding of Malinowski is primarily concerned with society and the role of religion in the social structure, phenomenological understanding centers its attention on religious structures and ideal archetypes. These structures and archetypes, we will see have ontological status, but are never fully realized in history. Religious structures are transhistorical means of understanding 'religion', or, for Eliade, the 'sacred'.

While Malinowski proceeded under a definition of religion which involved the supernatural, Eliade is reluctant to make clear his definition at all. The result is that his method proceeds under the essential-intuitional approach and the definition is therefore implicit and ambiguous rather than explicit. We have previously articulated the distinction between the essential-intuitional and the definitional-functional approaches. Eliade clearly falls into the former category. This has been considered in chapter one.

By declining to go to the definitional route, Eliade has opted for the intuitive point of departure. Religion, or the sacred, or man's reponse to the sacred, is something that can be identified without the need of a definition. How one is able to verify an authentic response to the sacred when it is intuitively identified, and how such a response can be distinguished from the demonic remains a problem. But the avoidance of a definitional starting point succeeds not in eliminating an ontological stance, but only in making that ontology less clear. It is still assumed that there is something out there that corresponds to the term 'religion' or 'the sacred', and also that the historian of religions can identify it intuitively. He can proceed to examine religion, reflecting on the nature of 'it' as he goes along.

In order to determine what this means for phenomenological understanding, we will consider Eliade's method with reference to symbolism, myth and ritual.

Phenomenological understanding of symbolism[57]

The meaning and methodological handling of symbolism participates in an ontology. By this we mean more than that symbolism implies an ontology for archaic man who uses the symbols.[58] An ontological stance is presupposed in the methodology itself.

The technical meaning of symbolism is more extensive than the mere assertion that a particular stone or a specific tree is a hierophany. Symbolism is the coherence of many symbols into a system which is implied in any one of them. For example, the symbolism of moon implies a system of hierophanies which cluster about the moon. The varied symbolism of snakes, women, etc., all have a lunar character, the moon acting as a symbol around which this symbolism seems to organize itself.

In the case of water symbolism, there is no such central symbol, but rather various water hierophanies. Nevertheless, they fit together into a coherent system. Water is the seed of things, the universal mother. There are water cosmogonies, the water of life, and the symbolism of immersion. Water symbolism involves the common element of water, but lacks a central hierophany such as unites lunar symbolism.[59]

We have only to recall the consistency of the symbolism of immersion in water (Baptism, the Flood, submersion of Atlantis), or purification by water (Baptism, funeral libations), of the time before the creation (the waters, the 'lotus', or the 'island', and so on), to recognize that there is a well-ordered system. This system is obviously implied in every water hierophany on however small a scale, but is more explicitly revealed through a symbol (as for instance 'the Flood' or Baptism'), and is only fully revealed in water symbolism as displayed in *all* the hierophanies.[60]

In the case of water symbolism, then, some hierophanies such as Baptism and the Flood are more clear in their intention. But there is, for Eliade, an overarching system which implies a meaning which is more comprehensive than any hierophany standing alone, and this system is *implied* in each particular hierophany. These systems manifest more clearly, more fully, and with greater coherence what each of the individual hierophanies intends. To interpret the hierophanies individualistically would be to lose their deepest meaning.

Eliade states that he is not arbitrarily deducing a symbolism that is not there. Nor is he rationalizing the materials so that they fit into such a preconceived system.[61] By examining many symbols, myths, rites, and by many cross references, he is able to find some clear hierophanies, some that are semi-veiled, and some that are obscure.[62] A study of these moves us toward a gradual understanding of what the symbol means. One can almost say that the clear hierophanies illuminate the obscure 'hierophanies'. The system is not something that is merely in the mind of the investigator, for each water hierophany actually implies the others.[63] Eliade does not seem to mean that men always *consciously* see in the symbol the implications of the whole logical system. The fact that some do not consciously understand all that is involved in a particular symbolism does not invalidate that symbolism.

For symbolism does not depend upon being understood; it remains consistent in spite of every corruption and preserves its structure even when it has been long forgotten, as witness those prehistoric symbols whose meaning was lost for thousands of years to be 'rediscovered' later.[64] This leads naturally into certain statements which Eliade has made regarding the subconscious or transconscious activity of man. The use of symbols comes before language and discursive reason and reveals the deepest aspects of reality. Hence the study of symbols assists us in a better understanding of man. This is an understanding of man as such, before he is particularized in history. Every historical man carries a great deal of this prehistoric humanity but the archetype of 'primordial man' is never fully realized in history. Eliade seems to suggest that it is in this subconscious of the race which explains the coherence that he finds in symbolism.

Eliade maintains that depth psychology has freed the historian of religions from any hesitation that he might have had about interpreting symbols, according to universally valid systems. Depth psychology has shown the survival of myths and symbols in the psyche of modern man irrespective of race or historical surroundings.

This internal logic of symbols raises a problem with far-reaching consequences: are certain zones of the individual or collective consciousness dominated by the *logos*, or are we concerned here with manifestation of a 'transconscious'? That problem cannot be resolved by depth-psychology alone, for the symbolisms which decipher the latter are the most part made up of scattered fragments and of the manifestations of the psyche in crisis, if not in a state of pathological regression. To grasp the authentic structures and functions of symbols, one must turn to the inexhaustable indices of the history of religions.[65]

It might be said that these statements which imply an ontology are merely attempts to account for the logical system of symbolisms which have been found by an examination of the phenomena. But that is not the end of the matter. Ethnologists are sometimes confused by Eliade's 'history of religions' since it is unlike any 'history' with which they are familiar. The confusion is due to the fact that for Eliade phenomenology of religion is a subdivision of the history of religions. It is an ahistorical approach which organizes material into structures irrespective of time and place. This method is best served if the phenomena are sufficiently removed from each other so that similarities in structure cannot be explained in terms of historical connections.

Eliade holds that it is not profitable to question the legitimacy of interpreting obscure symbols in the light of clear ones. Myths decay and symbols become secularized, but they never disappear. Even in the most profane society, they exist in some form.[66] But such assertions are based on an implied ontology which is nowhere philosophically defended. This ontological stance is most apparent when clear hierophanies are used to clarify the 'intention' of obscure 'hierophanies'. Such a hermeneutic is possible only if one assumes not only that the sacred has ontological status, but also that its structures (and hence the systems of symbolism) also have ontological status. Only on this basis could a *symbolism* reveal the meaning or 'intention' of a *symbol*.

Phenomenological understanding of myth

Eliade's method for understanding the religious meaning of myth is as transhistorical as his method for understanding symbols. Myths have structural unity even though they may be separated by centuries or continents.

Myths, as symbols, are hierophanies in that they reveal the sacred, the real. Eliade rejects the notion that myth is a fiction or illusion to be ignored or ridiculed. Nor ought the mythological to be removed from the existence of modern man. Indeed, modern man has been guilty of desacralizing the universe and is reaping his just deserts. For Eliade, myth is at least three things: sacred tradition, primordial revelation, and exemplary model.

Myths are sacred histories which take place at the beginning of time, and the actors are gods or culture heroes.

> The myth, then, is the history of what took place *in illo tempore*, the recital of what the gods or the semidivine beings did at the beginning of time.[67]

Mythological time is the time of the beginnings, and not historical time as such. Myths, then, do not belong to the profane, but to the sacred and hence to the real.

Myths are to be distinguished from false stories, for they are true stories which relate to reality. The Pawnee distinguish 'true stories' from 'false stories'.[68] In the former they include those stories which deal with the creation of the world and in which the actors are heavenly or supernatural beings. In the latter are included tales of national heroes, medicine men, or animals, tales in which less than gods are the actors.

The 'false stories' can be told anywhere and at any time. On the other hand the 'true stories' can only be told at a sacred time. Among many tribes they are not to be told before women and children, but only before the initiated.

...The truth describes the various and sometimes dramatic irruptions of the sacred into the world. This is why, among the primitives, myths cannot be recited without regard for time or place, but only during the seasons that are ritually richest (autumn, winter) or in the course of religious ceremonies – in short, during *a sacred period of time*.[69]

The archetypal myth is the cosmogonic myth or the myth of creation. From From the point of view of structure, myths of origins are to be homologized with the myths of creation. The point is that myths are always related to a creation, how something came into existence. Hence, origin myths continue the cosmogonic myth. For this reason some origin myths begin by recounting the cosmogony. For this same reason the great families and dynasties of Tibet are begun by rehearsing the birth of the Cosmos from an egg.[70] The Polynesian geneological chants begin the same way. The origin of medicines is also made a part of the cosmogonic myths. So it is 'that myth is always related to a 'creation', it tells how something came into existence, or how a pattern of behavior, an institution, a manner of working were established...'.[71]

The myths, because they are true, and because they relate the actions of the gods, become the exemplary models for all significant human activities. This is what is meant when a myth is called a paradigm or archetype. Frequently Eliade finds that when primitives are asked why they do something they respond that they do it either because the gods did it or because some ancestors did it 'in the beginning'. In the Old Testament, the sanction for the Sabbath rest is that Yahweh rested after his labors. This paradigmatic function is the main function of myths.

Hence the supreme function of the myth is to 'fix' the paradigmatic models for all rites and all significant human activities – eating, sexuality, work, eduacation, and so on. Acting as a fully responsible human being, man imitates the paradigmatic gestures of the gods, repeats their actions, whether in the case of a simple physiological function such as eating or of a social, economic, cultural, military, or other activity.[72] Here both Malinowski and Eliade agree – men in archaic cultures justify their actions in terms of the prior acts of the gods. However, the significance for the two is different. For Malinowski this provides social cohesion and the maintenance of tradition. For Eliade it points to the sanctification of the world.

This faithful repetition of divine models has a two-fold result: (1) by imitating the gods, man remains in the sacred, hence in reality; (2) by the continuous reactualization of paradigmatic divine gestures, the world is sanctified. Men's religious behavior contributes to maintaining the sanctity of the world.[73]

This is how religious man becomes truly human: by re-enacting the sacred history that is revealed in myths. *'One becomes truly a man only by conforming to the teaching of the myths, that is, by imitating the gods.'*[74]

We began by noting that Eliade's treatment of myth was transhistorical and that myths have structural unity even though separated by centuries and continents. Let us now turn to an illustration of how this is carried out. In a creation myth of the Society Islanders, the ancestor of the gods is said to have sat in his shell from eternity. Eliade points out that this cosmogonic egg is also found 'in India, Indonesia, Iran, Greece, Phoenicia, Latvia, Estonia, Finland, the Pangwe of West Africa, Central America and the west coast of South America...'.[75] Sometimes Maypoles are decorated with egg-shells, and in Persia coloured eggs are appropriate gifts for New Year. 'Clay eggs have been found in a great many tombs in Russia and Sweden; with good reason Arne sees them as emblems of immortality.'[76]

In all these cases, as in those we are coming to, the ritual power of the egg cannot be explained by any empirical or rationalist interpretation of the egg looked upon as a seed: it is fonded on the symbol embodied in the egg, which bears not so much upon birth as upon *rebirth* modelled on the creation of the world. Otherwise there could be no explanation for the important place eggs hold in the celebration of the New Year and the feasts of the dead.[77]

From one point of view, then, every myth is a cosmogonic myth since it either recounts the creation of the world, the origin of some thing, or renewal through rebirth by taking the participant back to the beginning of time. It will be abundantly clear what kinds of myths, rites, and practices are 'inexplicable' apart from Eliade's method by observing the breadth of his methodological net.

I will conclude with a few other instances of how the egg is used in ritual. There is, first, its role in the agricultural rituals still in use in modern times. To ensure that the grain would grow, Finnish peasants used to keep an egg in their pockets throughout the time of sowing, or place an egg in the plowed earth. The Estonians eat eggs during ploughing time 'to have strength', and the Swedes throw eggs down on ploughed fields. When the Germans are sowing flax they sometimes put eggs with it, or put an egg in the field, or eat eggs during the time of sowing. The Germans still have the custom of burying blessed Easter eggs in their fields. The Cheremisses and the Votyaks throw eggs up in the air before they start their sowing; on other occasions they would bury an egg among the furrows as an offering to the Earth Mother. The egg is at once an offering to the gods of the underworld and an offering used frequently in the cult of the dead. But whatever ritual pattern it is linked with, the egg never loses its primary meaning: it ensures the *repetition* of the act of creation which gave birth *in illo tempore* to living forms.[78]

It is difficult to verify such an interpretation of all these rituals. One either sees it or he doesn't. But without overarching religious structures which include symbols and myths and rituals, indeed all the activities of *homo religiosus*, such a transhistorical approach would be impossible.

Symbols are the most revelatory for archaic man since they are the most spontaneous. Certain mythologies such as those of ancient Greece, Rome and India, have undergone organization and literary development. Eliade feels it is better to begin with the myths of archaic societies. The reason for this is that the primitives' myths still reflect the primordial condition. These myths are still living and still justify and establish all human conduct. This is due to the more spontaneous state in which the myths are found.

The repetition of the myth enables one to return to the mythological times of the beginning. Hence the cosmogonic myth was repeated each New Year as the time was renewed. Rites cannot be performed unless their origin is known, that is, when they were performed for the first time. To repeat the origin of a disease is to cure it for it takes one back in mythological time to the beginning. Medical chants are often part of the cosmogonic myth. For archaic man, society cannot be repaired, it can only be recreated.

Myths keep alive in the consciousness of man the reality of another world. Recollection and re-enactment of the primordial even help archaic man to distinguish and hold to the real. Furthermore, the use of the myth creates confidence in man and makes an otherwise chaotic mass a meaningful Cosmos. 'Myth assures man that what he is about to do *has already been done*, in other words it helps him to overcome doubts as to the result of his undertaking.'[79] But one would be mistaken were he to chide archaic man for escapism. Actually, the mythological way is his way of grasping and transforming the world since he is participating in the creation anew.

> The imitation of the paradigmatic acts of the Gods, the Heroes, and the mythical ancestors does not produce an 'eternal repetition of the same thing', a total cultural immobility... But actually he is tirelessly conquering the world, organizing it, transforming the landscape of nature into a cultural milieu.[80]

Here, as in the interpretation of symbols, it is not necessary that persons be consciously aware of the depths of meaning contained in their mythical behavior. Eliade holds that some forms of mythical behavior still survive in our day. These are not survivals of an archaic mentality, but they indicate a human and religious dimension. The prestige of origins which has survived into the modern period is part of man's endeavor to get back to mythological time, the time of the beginning. In Europe, when an innovation is to be made it is conceived as a return to origins. The Reformation began as a return to the Bible and dreamed of recovering the experience of the primitive church. The passion for 'noble origin' explains the racist myth of 'Aryanism' which periodically gains currency in the West. Even though Marxism is eschatologically oriented, the classless society and the elimination of all historical tensions find their most exact precedent in the myth of the Golden Age which lies at the beginning of history.

Studies have brought out the mythological structures found in the mass media.

> The characters of the comic strips present the modern version of mythological or folklore Heroes. They incarnate the ideal of a large part of society, to such a degree that any change in their typical character or,

still worse, their death, will bring on veritable crises among their readers; the latter react violently, and protest by sending thousands of telegrams to the authors of the comic strips or the editors of the newspapers in which they appear. A fantastic character, Superman, has become extremely popular, especially because of his double identity; although coming from a planet destroyed by catastrophe, and possessing prodigious powers, Superman lives on earth in the modest guise of a journalist, Clark Kent; he is timid, unassertive, dominated by his colleague Lois Lane. This humiliating camouflage of a Hero whose powers are literally unlimited revives a wellknown mythological theme. In the last analysis, the myth of Superman satisfies the secret longings of modern man who, though he knows that he is a fallen, limited creature, dreams of one day proving himself an 'exceptional person', a Hero'.[81] Similar mythological behavior can be detected in the mythicization of public figures, or in the exemplary struggle between good and evil as depicted in detective novels.

Phenomenological understanding of rites
It should be apparent by now that there is no clear separation between symbols, myths, and rites. In practice they intersect as do the various religious structures. The various symbolic structures overlap and indeed participate in both myths and rituals. The egg is a symbol, is part of the cosmogonic myth, and becomes rite or ritual when it participates in meaningful activity on the part of *homo religiosus*.

However, to further clarify the distinctions between Malinowski and Eliade, it will be useful to consider rites of initiation. 'The term initiation in the most general sense denotes a body of rites and oral teachings whose purpose is to produce a decisive alteration in the religious and social status of the person to be initiated.'[82] Eliade recognizes, as did Malinowski, that in this rite the novice gains traditional knowledge and is introduced more fully into his culture. But the center of attention for Eliade is not the culture to which the supernatural and myths lend support. Instead, initiation is a part of what it means to sacralize the world. Culture is not merely reinforced through initiation, but it becomes sacralized and is one more illustration of archaic man's desire to live as completely as possible in the sacred. The contrast can be clearly seen in the following statement by Eliade.

In modern times we could say that initiation puts an end to the natural man and introduces the novice to culture. But for archaic societies, culture is not a human product, its origin is supernatural. Nor is this all. It is through culture that man reestablishes contact with the world of the Gods and other Supernatural Beings and participates in their creative energies.[83]

For Malinowski the religious dimension adds sanction to the traditional culture. For Eliade the introduction to the traditional culture and the sacred lore introduces man 'to the sacred history of the world and humanity'.[84]

In his understanding of rites of initiation, Eliade again chooses illustrations which are geographically and chronologically diverse.

> The ethnologist is concerned only with the societies that we call primitive, whereas the historian of religion will include the entire religious history of humanity in his field of investigation, from the earliest cults in palaeolithic times of which we have records down to modern religious movements.[85]

Hence he includes such diverse examples as Greco-Oriental mysteries, Tibetan Tantrism, the Scandinavian berserkers, and Australian puberty rites, to name only a few. But it is always his concern to ascertain the 'deeper' or transhistorical religious meaning which would never be acquired by examining only one cultural situation. And, given the ontological status of such universal structures, it is then possible to see meanings in a given initiation rite that it would never have revealed if it were taken alone.

Eliade finds three types of initiation: puberty rites, rites for entering a secret society, and rites for initiation into a mystical vocation (i.e. shaman). These, in spite of differences, participate in a common structure. But of these,

> *the puberty initiation represents above all the revelation of the sacred –
> and, for the primitive world, the sacred means not only everything that
> we now understand by religion, but also the whole body of the tribe's
> mythological and cultural traditions.*[86]

In the Australian puberty rites, the ceremonies begin with preparing the sacred ground. This ground, however represents the first camp of Baiamai, the Supreme Being. Since the ceremony takes place on this spot, it is a return to the mythological time of the beginnings. Furthermore, the details involved in the preparation are imitations of the gestures and acts of Baiamai. All of the gestures and operations and repetitions of exemplary models were first enacted by the founder of the ceremony in mythological time. Since these initiations are founded by the gods, man is returned to the primordial time whenever they are performed. And: 'This is true not only for the Australians, but for the entire primitive world.'[87] And so the preparation of the sacred ground has a meaning which is structurally consistent and which is religious rather than social.

> ...the Sacred ground plays an essential role in Australian initiation ceremonies because it represents the image of the primordial world as it was when the Divine Being was on earth.[88]

The second phase of such puberty initiation rites is the separation of the novices from their mothers and indeed from all women. Although the details of the separation differ according to historical variations, the initiatory instructions and ordeals are not to be witnessed by the women. As a Kurnai headsman reported: 'If a woman were to see these things, or hear what we tell the boys, I would kill her.'[89] The novices feel fear and experience darkness. They are told that they will be captured and killed by Divine Beings. All this is an experience of death as a prerequisite to rebirth.

> This experience of darkness, of death, and of the nearness of Divine Beings will be continually repeated and deepened throughout the initiation... But it is important to emphasize that the very first act of the ceremony already implies the experience of death, for the novices are violently flung into an unknown world where the presence of Divine Beings is sensed through the terror that they inspire.[90]

The separation from the mothers represents the violent break with childhood 'which is at once the maternal and female world and the child's state of irresponsibility and happiness, of ignorance and asexuality'.[91] The novices thus die to childhood and will be returned as men, for even the mothers believe not only that the sons will be killed and eaten by the divinity, but will also be resuscitated as grown men.

> The maternal universe was that of the profane world. The universe that the novices now enter is that of the sacred world. Between the two, there is a break, a rupture of continuity. Passing from the profane to the sacred world in some sort implies the experience of death; he who makes the passage dies to one life in order to gain access to another.[92]

Hence we have here an extension of cosmogonic myth in which one is created anew.

A third phase of these initiatory rites is the segregation of the novices in the bush or in another isolated spot where they are instructed in the sacred lore of the tribe. Sometimes the initiates will live in the bush for six or seven months, being visited by tutors from time to time. During this period there are numerous prohibitions, some of which are of a dietary nature.

A fourth phase involves 'certain operations performed on the novices, usually circumcision, the extraction of a tooth, or subincision, but sometimes scarring or pulling out the hair'.[93] The suffering which follows such operations is an expression of initiatory death. But there are other ordeals which are equally significant. Some novices are ordered not to go to sleep until late at night. This is 'above all to show proof of will and spiritual strength; to remain awake is to be conscious, present in the world, responsible'.[94] Dietary prohibitions and the ritual of not touching the food with one's fingers is also significant. Sometimes the guardian of the novice will put food into the novice's mouth for the entire initiatory period. 'The inference would seem to be that the novice is regarded as a newborn infant and hence cannot feed himself without help.'[95] Certain prohibitions against speech carry the two-fold meaning of the return to death and to earliest infancy. Sometimes initiates are blindfolded or allowed to walk only with their heads bent.

> Darkness is a symbol of the other world, whether the world of death or of the fetal state. Whatever meaning we give to segregation in the bush – whether we see it as a death or as a return to the prenatal condition – it is clear that the novice is no longer in the profane world.[96]

Malinowski would point to the ordeals as part of the impressive setting in which the traditional lore is taught, thus resulting in societal cohesion. For him the gods add to the seriousness with which such an event would be taken. But Eliade's concern is not with the continuance of society, but with the transhistorical religious meaning of an event.

But all these prohibitions – fasting, silence, darkness, complete suppression of sight or its restriction to the ground between the novice's feet – also constitute so many ascetic exercises. The novice is forced to concentrate, to meditate. Hence the various physical ordeals also have a spiritual meaning. The neophyte is at once prepared for the responsibilities of adult life and progressively awakened to the life of the spirit. For the ordeals and restrictions are accompanied by instruction through myths, dances, pantomimes. The physical ordeals have a spiritual goal –

to introduce the youth into the tribal culture, to make him 'open' to spiritual values.[97]

As with symbols and myths, so with rites of initiation. Modern man, who has desacralized the universe, possesses only survivals of initiatory motifs. But he cannot completely eliminate the theme which pervades his dream experiences and his unconscious. This also supports the point that we have already seen with symbolism and myths: religious structures have ontological status and cannot therefore be destroyed, only mutilated or badly camouflaged.

But there is more: the imaginative activity and the dream experiences of modern man continue to be pervaded by religious symbols, figures, themes. As some psychologists delight in repeating, the unconscious is religious. From one point of view it could be said that in the man of desacralized societies, religion has become 'unconscious'; it lies buried in the deepest strata of his being; but this by no means implies that it does not continue to perform an essential function in the economy of the psyche.[98]

We began our discussion of Eliade's phenomenological method by stating that it was primarily concerned with religious structures. It might be countered that this does not mean that it is uninterested in religious people. For, the only way Eliade proposes to adequately understand religious man is by understanding the structures in which he participates. However, the emphasis is certainly on the structures. Participants or believers need not be aware of the 'depth of meaning' which Eliade knows is contained in their symbols, myths, or rites. It is true that Eliade's goal is to understand *homo religiosus*. But *homo religiosus* is not an historical but an archetypal religious man. Historical persons participate in this archetype to varying degrees, even though no one fully embodies it nor does anyone entirely cover it. Hence the statements of religious men about the meanings of their rites or symbols is secondary to the way in which the symbols fit into universal structures. And, individuals are understood in terms of these universal structures and not in terms of their religious individuality.

While no one person is the complete embodiment of *homo religiosus*, archaic man comes closest to this model of authentic existence. Eliade begins by convincing us that we should be prepared to admit that *homo religiosus* has had a tendency to extend hierophanies indefinitely. Almost everything has been a hierophany at one time or another to someone or other. This is particularly true for archaic man. But when it is suggested that modern man is poorer because his cosmos has been desacralized, because the human body or the process of eating is no longer a sacrament, a shift has been effected – a shift that is made possible only because an ontological basis has already been posited. If not before, at least here it is clear that Eliade is not dealing merely with what men have held to be sacred, but with the structures of the sacred. His focal point is not only the subjective, but also the objective and hence ontological. Not only are the hierophanies which he describes hierophanies for those involved, but they are *in fact* hierophanies. One would normally expect further argumentation when a shift is made from the apparently descriptive to the normative. Here, however, an ontology has been posited from the start.

Once one sees 'the sacred' or 'religion' as an ontological reality and once one operates as though its structures are also ontologically real, having identified these structures one has discovered reality. It then follows that those whose lives are lived in the sacred as completely as possible are the most authentic since they exist closest to reality.

It might be worth pointing out that not all phenomenologists of religion have taken Eliade's step of seeing archaic man as the most authentic.

Modern man has a clearer view of what is genuinely religious, is more able to distinguish the religious from the secular and makes higher demands as to the quality of religion.[99]

It is not the lack of an ontological basis that pushes Bleeker in a different direction at this point, but it is because his intuitive identification of religion differs from Eliade's. This might lead one to question the notion that we all know what religion is and can readily identify it, even though we have definitional difficulties.

Eliade maintains that it falls within the realm of the historian of religions to articulate a systematic and theoretical interpretation of the religious facts that he finds as a phenomenologist.

The second prejudice of certain historians of religions, that you must turn to another 'specialist' for a world-wide and systematic interpretation of religious facts, is probably to be explained by the philosophical timidity of a great number of scholars.[100]

In a footnote, Eliade laments the fact that 'general theories' which have dominated the history of religions from its beginnings have been the work of linguists, anthropologists, sociologists, and philosophers.[101] These are bold statements when one remembers the concern of other historians of religions to disassociate themselves from the work of theologians and philosophers of religion.[102] To urge the historian of religions to philosophize at this point is to add little new to Eliade's method. An ontology has been implied from the start. What is more surprising is that this prior ontology is seldom if ever recognized as such. The result is that it is assumed that the philosophizing will come at the end of an examination of the given religions, when it would have been logically more appropriate in this method to find it at the beginning. For, if the ontological dimension of Eliade's phenomenological approach to the sacred is not validly supported, the conclusion remains equally unsupported. But Eliade thinks the philosophizing must conclude the study. If one fails to philosophize at this point,

> ...this amounts to saying that the historian of religions hesitates to complete his *preparatory work* as a philologist and as a historian through an effort of *understanding*, which, to be sure, presupposes an act of thinking.[103]

Eliade laments the fact that the discipline of the history of religions has had a rather modest role in influencing modern culture.[104] This is largely because historians of religions have been too cautious. Having remained specialized, they fail to recognize the unlimited possibilities that are open to the history of religions. In attempting to remain scientific, thereby avoiding broad generalizations, historians of religions have paid the price of creativity. Eliade urges the historian of religions to go beyond the mere comprehending of religious facts to the level of philosophizing.[105] By this kind of thought the history of religions can help to create cultural values.[106] The reason why this does not happen often enough is that the majority of historians of religions defend themselves against the messages contained in the documents they study. Eliade is suggesting more than a spontaneous enlivening of the subconscious of modern man, for if his theoretical structures are real, this would simply happen apart from the philosophizing efforts of historians of religions.

It is true that artificial disciplinary barriers have been erected so that if one wants to wear his label with cultic dignity, whether as 'historian of religions" 'anthropologist', or 'theologian', there are some things that he is well advised not to do. But there is no valid reason why Eliade should be excluded from the possibility of philosophizing, or theologizing for that matter. There are various stages in Eliade's method which are philosophical – at the point of departure as well as at the point of destiny. And at all points at which ontology is assumed such philosophizing becomes essential. A failure to recognize the ontological point of departure and the assumption that he is beginning with the given religions which we can all readily identify without the need of a definition leads Eliade to miss the fact that wherever an ontological stance is introduced, philosophical argumentation is needed. It must be said that if historians of religions are going to engage in a phenomenological approach such as Eliade's, and if they are going to be called upon to develop the theoretical and philosophical implications of their findings, then simply being 'most familiar with the religious facts' is insufficient preparation.[107] One who engages in such work also needs ability in philosophical method. Whatever theories or conclusions flow from the work of those who attempt to achieve phenomenological understanding will be acceptable and valid only to the extent to which one's descriptions are accurate *and* to the extent to which (where applicable) his normative stages are adequately supported.

We have found that both the methods of Malinowski and Eliade have involved metaphysical positions and that neither seemed more eager than the other to defend the metaphysical dimensions of their systems with the appropriate philosophical or theological reasoning. With the level of functional understanding, however, we found that it was possible to divest the method of Malinowski's 'postulates' and still use the method heuristically. This has been cogently argued by Merton. The question now arises as to whether it would be possible to empty Eliade's phenomenological method of its ontological 'postulates' and continue to use it as a level of understanding. In the case of Eliade's phenomenological method, we are forced to answer in the negative. Here, if one eliminates the methapysical, he eliminates the transhistorical religious structures. And, the elimination of the transhistorical religious structures eliminates the possibility of finding a transhistorical religious meaning in a symbol or myth or rite. Without its implied ontology, this method falls to the ground and becomes at best *a means of classifying data*. But classification itself is little more than a scholarly filing system which enables us to know where to find a given thing at a given time. Hence, without positing ontological structures the phenomenological method does not offer a distinct method of understanding, merely a means of classification.

This being said, it remains to be said that the phenomenological method is a legitimate level of understanding to the extent to which one is convinced of the reality of the transhistorical structures and archetypes. These cannot be supported by merely citing historically derived data. For it is the organization of that data into transhistorical structures which makes the method distinct. And, one has no right to do that until some evidence for the existence of the transhistorical structures has been offered. Empirical evidence cannot be used for this task. One must reason philosophically or theologically. These transhistorical structures are not empirically verifiable because they are not empirically falsifiable. There is no way that an examination of historical data will show that they do not exist. It may lead one to identify them differently from the way that Eliade does. But that does not touch at the heart of the problem, which is whether it is legitimate to interpret some material in the light of other material because there exist transhistorical structures in which both participate. Since there are cryptic as well as apparent hierophanies, it follows that those items which do not explicitly identify their place in a religious structure can be assigned such a place. The weight of this method is that it enables one to 'understand' those religious symbols, myths, or rites which do not explicitly tell us their meaning. But, since this is the case, there is no way to verify if such 'cryptic' hierophanies actually do fit into the transhistorical structures at the places where the phenomenologist says they do, or whether they fit into any such structures, or finally, whether such structures do indeed exist.

It is difficult to improve on the observation of Willard Oxtoby.

Analogous in a sense to Gestalt psychology, the eidetic vision constitutes a confident, self-validating sense that the pattern which one has distilled represents the real essentials of the data... There is nothing outside one's intuitive grasp of a pattern which validates that pattern. The phenomenologist is obliged simply to set forth his understanding as a whole, trusting that his reader will enter into it. But there is no procedure stated by which he can compel a second phenomenologist to agree with the adequacy and incontrovertibility of his analysis, unless the second phenomenologist's eidetic vision happens to be the same as the first's. For this reason phenomenological expositions of religion are in fact very personal appreciations of it, akin more to certain forms of literary and aesthetic criticism than to the natural or even the social sciences.[108]

In short, the phenomenological understanding of religion, as exhibited in the work of Eliade, will appear useful to all those who share his ontological stance. Whether this sharing is the result of being convinced by philosophical arguments or because of a favorable emotional response to an organizational principle for an overwhelming mass of data only indicates the degree to which a scholar demands critical evidence for his religious commitments. But the phenomenology of Eliade is a normative level of understanding. It could well have been considered alongside Hendrik Kraemer, Hans Küng, and S. Radhakrishnan. This level is considered separately because of its wide acceptance among historians of religions and in order to clarify the limitations of the phenomenological level of understanding.

Of course, as with all normative understanding, if the norm proves erroneous, one no longer has understanding at all, but rather misunderstanding.[109] Hence, if the universal religious structures on which Eliade bases his understanding of the religious data should turn out to be non-existent, then this approach would result in misunderstanding as well.

However, if cogent arguments are forthcoming in support of the implied ontology, the phenomenological level stands as a legitimate level of understanding. Heinz Robert Schlette has accused Eliade of comparing before he has adequately understood what he compares.

In the words of M. Eliade too, precipitate comparisons and identifications are found. For example Eliade who, of course, deals with religions by the methods and from the point of view of ethnology, theory of archetypes, morphology of civilizations, theory of mythology and mysticism, considers he must include Christian baptism (the 'historical' element having deliberately been put in parenthesis), in a list with 'Polynesian, American, ancient Greek and ancient oriental myths and rites' in order 'to throw light on the structure of water hierophanies'.[110]

Schlette misunderstands Eliade's method. His method implies that, because of the ontological status of religious structures, one reaches phenomenological understanding precisely through placing items together which are not identical but structurally homologous.

C. PERSONAL UNDERSTANDING: WILFRED CANTWELL SMITH

If the focus of Malinowski's concern was on society, and Eliade's emphasis was on religious structures, Wilfred Cantwell Smith's primary interest is in religious persons. As early as his inaugural address at McGill University, he characterized historians of religions as 'flies crawling on the surface of a goldfish bowl, making accurate and complete observations on the fish inside... and indeed contributing much to our knowledge of the subject; but never asking themselves, and never finding out, how it feels to be a goldfish'.[111]

In another early statement he proposed that 'the study of religion is the study of persons'.[112] This does not mean that texts, rites, and rituals, temples, etc. are to be ignored. It does mean, hoever, that such are examined with the explicit purpose of understanding religious persons.

The traditional form of Western scholarship in the study of other men's religion was that of an impersonal presentation of an 'it'. The first great innovation in recent times has been the personalization of the faiths observed so that one finds a discussion of a 'they'. Presently the observer becomes personally involved, so that the situation is one of a 'we' talking about a 'they'. The next step is dialogue, where 'we' talk to 'you'. If there is listening and mutuality, this may become that 'we' talk *with* 'you'. The culmination of this process is when 'we all' are talking *with* each other about 'us'.[113]

Such a concern for religious persons is also found in Smith's method of verification. No statement about a religion is valid unless it can be acknowledged by that religion's believers. This is valid in principle for all historical studies which attempt to get at the faith of persons. But, it is most easily applied among living religions where direct confrontation is possible. Smith is aware of this limitation when he states:

There are complications regarding historical change; I recognize that a religion develops, whereas few believers do recognize this, so that what once was true about it may no longer be so, and the insider can speak authoritatively only for the present.[114]

The attempt to understand the faiths of persons has been hindered by the use of certain categories and questions that have been applied by historians of religions. Among these, the most commonly used are the terms 'religion' and 'religions'.

Neither religion in general nor any one of the religions, I will contend, is in itself an intelligible entity, a valid object of inquiry or of concern either for the scholar or for the man of faith.[115]

It is Smith's purpose in *The Meaning and End of Religion*, to clear away the faulty structuring of questions based on the above terminology, and to offer in its place another possibility. Our language betrays that we are accustomed to thinking that there is something in human life and society that can be called 'religion'. Our analysis of Malinowski and Eliade, and our prior discussion of the essential-intuitional approach seems to indicate that this is as true of the scholar as it is of the man of affairs. It is the assumption that 'religion' is a something which enables people to blame 'religion' for society's ills or praise it for its benefits, as though 'it' is *something* to be blamed or praised.

In addition to this we have been accustomed to thinking in terms not only of 'religion' but also of 'religions' which are forms of the former and to which we give such names as 'Hinduism', 'Buddhism', 'Judaism', 'Christianity', and 'Islam'. It is Smith's contention that there is nothing which corresponds to such terminology. There is no entity called 'religion' since religion is not an object, but a vivid and personal confrontation with God. The difficulty which people have had in defining religion may indicate that it is a term which ought to be dropped. Religion is 'a distorted concept not really corresponding to anything definite or distinctive in the objective world'.[116] Smith agrees that the phenomenon which is described as 'religious' exists, but not 'religion'. In *The Faith of Other Men*,[117] he speaks not so much of other religions, but of the *faith* of other men. Hence, instead of dealing with Hinduism, Buddhism, Islam, he discusses the faith of 'Hindus', 'Buddhists', 'Muslims', 'Chinese', and 'Christians and Jews'.

For this reason the question 'What is the nature of religion?' is to be avoided. As Smith puts it:

> I suggest that an understanding of the variegated and evolving religious situation of mankind can proceed, and indeed perhaps can proceed only if that question in that form be set aside or dropped as inept.[118]

In attempting to set the stage for his argument, Smith sketches the history of the word 'religion'. He is well aware that an historical treatment is not sufficient to substantiate his argument, but the historical sketch has a two-fold function: It assists in clarifying Smith's position, and it gives him comfort to know that he is not alone in his position.

Smith finds that the adjectival use of the word has been employed more frequently than the substantive. This, he feels, supports the notion that in the early Christian period and before, the important thing was piety (or a religious attitude), rather than 'religion'. Christianity introduced a novelty into the Greek world by carrying on a certain we-they exclusivism which was also beginning to take shape among the Jews. In the New Testament this reification has not yet taken place. When the author of the book of James said that 'religion that is pure and undefiled before God and the Father is this...', he was describing a quality of the experience of the truly religious man. He was not contrasting 'our' religion which is pure with 'theirs' which is corrupt.

Although his historical discussion is more complete than our review of it can be, his point is made quite clear in the cases of Augustine and John Calvin. Augustine consciously undertook to explicate the notion of *religio*. He entitled his work *De Vera Religione*. What is meant by this is basic to Smith's point. Our modern use of the word shines through when translators want to render this title 'On The True Religion', and suppose that since the writer was a Christian, he would also believe that the true religion was Christianity. A closer translation would be 'On True Religion' which means 'On Proper Piety' or 'On Genuine Worship'. Augustine argues at length that *vera religione* means worship of the true God. The book hardly mentions Christianity, 'and culminates in a warm, reverberating and sustained affirmation of a personal relation to that transcendent God, "from whom, through whom, and in whom are all things. To Him be glory for ever and ever, Amen".'[119]

> For this writer 'religion' is no system of observances or beliefs, nor an historical tradition, institutionalized or susceptible of outside observation. Rather it is a vivid and personal confrontation with the splendor and love of God.

The Church, for him, exists in order to make this relationship possible.[120] The end is mystical. *Religio* is the bond which unites men with God. It depicts a relationship between God and man which ought to subsist and which was never absent from the beginning of mankind until now. The difficulty is that religion was reified and turned into an object. Smith holds that the concern of religious man is with God, the concern of the observer is with religion. 'In any case, it is not entirely foolish to suggest that the rise of the concept "religion" is in some ways correlated with the decline in the practice of religion itself.'[121]

When Calvin's *Christianae Religionis Institutio* is rendered 'Institutes of the Christian Religion' a similar misunderstanding is created. 'Institutio' means instruction, and *religio*, far from being one of the religions, refers to the sense of piety which prompts a man to worship. For Calvin the material described and discussed in his 'Institutes' was not religion, but rather things which he hoped would guide men into a personal and worshipful recognition of God. This he called '*Christiana religio*'.

A century later men were calling by this name not that personal vision but the matters such as he set forth to lead to it: the system of beliefs and practices, considered as a system, irrespective of whether or not they elicited in the human heart a genuine fear of and love for God. The difference is momentous.[122]

So, the system becomes 'the Christian Faith', and since there are other systems as well, one arrives at the position that there are different religions which can be considered as true or false in the intellectual sense. This is a transition from a personal orientation to 'depersonalized intellectual systematization'. So there is the development of the plural 'religions' which is not possible so long as *religio* is something which is in men's hearts, and then there is the generic concept of 'religion' to 'designate as an external entity the total system or sum of all systems of beliefs, or simply the generalization that they are there'.[123]

In the ninteenth century the idea arose that one could find the 'essence of religion' or the essence of a religion such as Christianity. In 1851 Ludwig Feuerbach published *The Essence of Religion* and in 1861 *The Essence of Christianity*. Smith feels that the important point is not what the essence was suggested to be in each case, but that it was believed that religion and the religions have an essence.

Ever since the hunt has been on. The idea was widely accepted that religion is a something with a definite and fixed form, if only one could find it.[124]

Smith finds the reified meaning of religion irrelevant to the non-civilized peoples who simply perform their rites and relate their myths without constructing a system and naming it. When it comes to the ancient cultures of Egypt, Greece, Rome, or Iran, we have had to content ourselves with such designations as 'Roman Religion'. Scholars in each of these fields commonly say that the modern distinction made between religion and other aspects of society do not exist in the cultures they study.

'Hinduism' is a particularly false conceptualization. The term 'Hindu' was first used as a religious designation by the Muslims after they had invaded India in the second millenium A. D. It was used to designate those whom they had conquered, and at the same time included what has since been labelled

Jainism and Buddhism. Even today it is difficult for census takers to distinguish between 'Hindus' and 'animists'.

My objection to the term 'Hinduism', of course, is not on the grounds that nothing exists. Obviously an enormous quantity of phenomenon is to be found that this term covers. My point, and I think that this is the first step that one must take towards understanding something of the vision of the Hindus, is that the mass of religious phenomenon that we shelter under the umbrella of that term, is not a unity and does not aspire to be. It is not an entity in any theoretical sense, let alone any practical one.[125] The Chinese do not fit into religious systems any better. Westerners are sometimes confused when they learn that a Chinese may be and probably is a 'Confucian', a 'Buddhist', and a 'Taoist'. They find it difficult to see how one can be a member of three religions simultaneously. The answer is to be found in the unnatural conceptualization that is used in the West. There is no term for 'Buddhists' or 'Taoists' in Chinese. The reason for this, holds Smith, is that while schools of thought exist in China, closed communities never developed around them. There are no parties with such clear-cut boundries which exist when one 'joins the Christian Church'. 'To ask a census-taker how many Chinese are Buddhist is rather like asking one how many Westerners are Aristotelian or pragmatist.'[126] It is for this reason that no satisfactory answer has been given to the question of whether Pali Buddhism or Confucianism is a religion. The Chinese or Indians never asked the question, and, the way it is phrased, the West will never be able to answer to it.[127]

After World War II, a Japanese census indicated that the total number of 'Buddhists', 'Shintoists' and 'Christians' amounted to half again as many people as were on the islands. The clear-cut distinction between 'religions' did not exist. The term 'Shinto' means 'the way of the Gods'. Apparently the term itself did not come into use in Japan until the thirteenth century. This 'way of the Gods' is not a unified way at all.

> There has been no systematic pattern, either in practice or in history. 'Shinto' does not refer to an ideal; but at best to a congeries of disparate ideals and complex actualities.[128]

Is Shinto a religion? The question was first framed in Japan in the nineteenth century. It was asked by outsiders, and the Japanese answered 'No'.

Islām is a special case in that the Arabic word *dīn* is roughly equivalent to 'religion' and Muslims see their religion as having a name which was revealed by Allāh. But even here, a word study shows that there has been a growing tendency to reify, a tendency that was only slight in the *Qur'an*. A statistical study shows that the word Islām is used much less in the *Qur'an* than other terms of a more personal and dynamic nature. And, in numerous places the term 'Islām' can and often must be interpreted as a decisive personal act rather than as a name for a religious system. Islām ultimately means submission, obedience, commitment, the recognition of one's finitude before the majesty of God. If one says in English 'I am not a Muslim', the point is clear. But if one were to take it in its Arabic sense it would be construed as 'I do not submit to God . And so Smith puts it:

> I am not a Muslim with a capital M in the technical English sense of belonging to the institutionalized Islamic community system, partly by by accident of birth and partly because the chief tradition of those who are members of that community system and I differ as to how best one knows what God's will is; but we do not disagree in our acceptance, our *Islām*, of such commands as we do apprehend.[129]

A study of the use of the words Islām and Imān (faith) in book titles indicated to Smith a growing reification since the nineteenth century, and a need felt by Muslims to engage in apologetic defenses of their faith in the light of attacks from the West.

> Our conclusion is that the Islamic has been in some ways from the first the most reified of all man's living religious movements, that it has at its birth and throughout been subject to massive reifying pressures; and yet that like all the others it began (was proclaimed in the Qur'an) as a ringing personal summons to men and women to have faith in God and to commit themselves wholeheartedly to his commands, and that the institutions and conceptualized systems of what is now called Islam have been the result of that faith and commitment.[130]

There are two basic objections to the utilization of such concepts as 'religion' or 'religions'. The first objection is that the concept is offered by the outsider and is an inadequate concept for the believer, the man of faith. For the insider Heaven and Hell are parts of one's universe, places into which one is likely to step. But to the observer they are merely items in the believer's mind. The reified concepts of 'religion' and the 'religions' arose to serve the outsider's purpose, but they are inadequate for the insider or man of faith. The conclusion is that if the concepts are inadequate for the man of faith, they can only be mis-

leading for the outsider, for to use a concept which does not describe the
actual attitudes of the believer will tend to disguise the fact that he actually
does believe. For Christians, for example, it is only as faith in God has
weakened that men have been concerned with 'Christianity'. Their relationship
to Christ having lapsed, they turn to religion for solace.

Such a notion is a kind of blasphemy, to those whose faith is sensitive.
One has even reached a point today where some Christians can speak of
believing in Christianity (instead of believing in God and in Christ); of
preaching Christianity (instead of preaching good news, salvation,
redemption); of practicing Christianity (instead of practicing love). Some
even talk of being saved by Christianity, instead of by the only thing that
could possibly save us, the anguish and love of God.[131]

If the first reason for the rejection of such terminology is that it does not
reflect the situation of the religious person we are seeking to understand, the
second is the nature of history. Such concepts presuppose that there is
definiteness all around, whereas 'every historian knows that in fact there is
flux'.[132] In history no such thing as 'Christianity' or 'Buddhism' or any other
religion exists, for these concepts are static and history is change.

Neither the believer nor the observer can hold that there is anything on
earth that can legitimately be called 'Christianity' or 'Shintoism' or
'religion' without recognizing that if such a thing existed yesterday, it
existed in a somewhat different form the day before. If it exists in one
country (or village) it exists in somewhat different form in the next.
The concepts were formed before the ruthlessness of historical change
was recognized, in all its disintegrating sweep. They have in practice been
abandoned as awareness has grown. It is time now definitely to reject
them theoretically, as inherently inept.[133]

One can define 'Hinduism' as an ideal, but not as an historical entity.
Hinduism merely refers to a variety of facts. Smith is not contending merely
that it is difficult to define 'Hinduism', or 'Taoism', or 'Buddhism'. To him
this is self-evident. What he means is that it is 'in principle impossible, and
almost perverse'.[134] He recognizes that what men have called religions do
exist, but contends that they exist in such profuseness that one cannot capture
them under static concepts such as 'religion' or 'religions'. 'What has been
called Christianity is, so far as history is concerned, not one thing but millions
of things, and hundreds of millions of persons.'[135]

There are numerous metaphysical questions which are difficult to solve and the historian of religions will make progress in the study of man's religions if he uses a method which will enable him to get on with it by passing over such questions. According to Smith, we not only cannot, but we must not begin by trying to solve the question of the nature of religion, or the question of the relationship between transcendence and the world. Metaphysically and theologically the relationship between the latter two is not clear, but it is clear historically speaking. As far as the historian is concerned, the connecting link is man. The history of religion and religions is actually the history of man's participation in an evolving context of observable actualities, and in a something, not directly observable by historical scholarship'.[136] History distorts reality if it omits either the mundane or the transcendent.

Smith suggests that instead of religion or religions, we work with two concepts: cumulative tradition and faith. The link between the two is the living person. Here one can see the emphasis that Smith places on the fact that the study of 'religion' is the study of persons. By 'faith' Smith means personal faith. '...Let it stand for an inner religious experience or involvement of a particular person; the impingement on him of the transcendent, putative or real.'[137] By 'cumulative tradition' he means:

> ...the entire mass of overt objective data that constitute the historical
> deposit, as it were, of the past religious life of the community in question:
> temples, scriptures, theological systems, dance patterns, legal and other
> social institutions, conventions, moral codes, myths, and so on; anything
> that can be and is transmitted from one person, one generation, to an-
> other, and that an historian can observe.[138]

Smith deals with some of the ways and modes through which faith expresses itself: art, community, social institutions, character, ritual and morality, words and ideas. Nevertheless, beyond all this, to be religious is ultimately a personal act. 'Theology is part of the traditions, is part of this world. Faith lies beyond theology, in the hearts of men. Truth lies beyond faith, in the heart of God.'[139] The cumulative tradition, then, is the result of the faith of men in the past and at least the partial cause of faith in the future.

While it is not possible to observe faith, 'we should be able to arrive at a point where we can understand, not with complete assurance but with reasonable confidence, and not fully but in significant part, what the faith of other persons, other groups, even other ages, is and has been'.[140] This is the new challenge for 'Comparative Religion'. Some effort has already been exerted on the 'cumulative tradition'. The next step is to make known the personal faith of the men whom those traditions have served.

Smith's method can be illustrated by describing his treatment of the Burmese *Shin Byu* ceremony.[141] This is an initiation rite for Buddhist boys which takes place at the age of puberty or earlier. Smith's analysis of this rite is not concerned with the role it plays in preserving a traditional set of values and in preserving societal cohesiveness (Malinowski), nor in the fact that in re-enacting a rite first performed by the Buddha, one is participating in an archetypal experience (Eliade), but in what it means to the persons who participate in this rite.

The *Shin Byu* ceremony is a re-enactment of the 'Going Out' of the Buddha, or his 'Great Renunciation' when he left his palace luxury to become a mendicant. In Burma it is an exciting moment filled with festivities. The child is dressed in princely garb, his family and friends celebrate his coming of age. At a certain point in the ceremony he takes off his princely garb, dons the saffron robe of the monk, and enters the monastery. His stay there may be only for a few weeks, or he may remain there for his schooling or possibly take up the monastic career as his own.

In attempting to analyze what this ceremony means to the people involved it is necessary to say that the ceremony symbolizes something that is greater than man and hence cannot be fully apprehended. But, first, there are the *parents* of the boy. For them this must be a moving experience, when they hand their son over from their personal charge to that of the community.

> They are enacting the transition by which he *becomes* (that word is so disalarmingly simple!), becomes no longer the child of a Buddhist, which is one thing, profoundly meaningful, but a Buddhist, which is another.[142]

For them the child is not forsaking their religious concerns, but is identifying himself with the Buddha as they themselves had previously done. He is not in their eyes, leaving to set out on a career entirely his own.

> Instead, they see him as humanly independent, yet oriented in what they regard as the cosmically right direction, free of their control but accepting as they have done in free commitment the guidance of a transcending wisdom.[143]

As for what this ceremony means to the boy himself, Smith is uncertain.

As for the boy himself, I will not try to speculate as to what goes on in his mind, at either the conscious or unconscious level. How much he personally has been moved, in his home or at previous village ceremonies, by the stories of the Buddha; how sensitive he has been, in such contacts with the monastery of the monks as he has had, to the numinous quality of life, crystallized in these sanctities – such things will vary, of course, from boy to boy. How deep an impression the day will make on him; how seriously he takes the moment when he doffs the splendid gala attire, to take on instead the austere garb of the monastery; how touched he may be with some spiritual overtones or simply with nostalgia or mischief, as he says good-bye to his parents and sets his face towards the monastery – I leave you to judge.[144] The boy's later development through the years will be more determinative as to whether he will minimize or forget the significance of this event or whether he will increasingly come to know the meaning behind the symbol.

But this ceremony is not merely the possession of the individuals involved. It is also the possession of the social community and the religious order. Everyone who participates is reminded that there exists an 'enduring quality that transcends the mundane, and lifts us, or can lift us, out of the utterly contingent; and that this quality is moral'.[145] The participants are not creating the ceremony, but are orienting themselves toward the Buddha and affirming that the moral law is not merely their own creation, not the mere tradition of the community, but was given to them by someone else. The social re-enactment makes it possible for persons to become religiously involved again and again.

This point applies to everyone individually, and must be re-enacted over again as each new generation, each new person, comes along. It applies to every society, so that the whole community participates in each one of its members' personal involvement; and does so again and again.[146] While the social dimension is recognized, religion is not understood on the level of social function (Malinowski). Instead, the social dimension is seen as an opportunity for persons to participate 'in each one of its members' personal involvement'.

The significance of this event is, for Smith, the personal meaning for the faith of persons. And, although he is not ignoring the historical connection with the renunciation of the Buddha many years before, his concern is not so much with that historical event as with what the living persons make of it.

The fact that the participants relate this event to the Buddha offers an assurance since the Buddha did achieve Buddhahood. That is significant, but the
emphasis is on what this might mean to the living persons.

I wonder whether you see the importance that I do in the living assurance
here that someone has shown the way, having travelled it. Therefore
this is not a guess, but a discovery; not a groping, but a joyous affirmation.
Now, this remains true, and you and I can recognize it as such, quite
apart from any question of whether or not we are Buddhists. Our
capacity to see its significance and even its validity does not turn on our
accepting any doctrine about the Buddha. One might almost be tempted
to say that this aspect of the ceremony is made true not by what the
Buddha accomplished, but by the faith of men in his having accomplished
it.[147]

Smith is not interested in raising the normative question of whether the
Buddha did achieve Buddhahood, or what his real significance was in later
history. He is interested in the role that this belief plays in the faith of men.

We need not agree with them on any metaphysical role that Buddha
played in the past, in actual history; and yet we may recognize the metaphysical role that he is playing today in the lives of these men. And we
may recognize the significance of their faith – and this faith even an
outsider may share – that such a role is ideally there, to be filled. What
am suggesting is that there is a metaphysical truth in these Buddhists
faith, which is independent of the historical truths of their belief.[148]

Perhaps Smith's closing remark to this chapter of his book indicates what
his method is attempting to accomplish.

I close, then, hoping that perhaps this brief presentation may have helped
you to feel that once you have learned the form, you yourself could
reasonably participate, at least imaginatively, in such a ceremony as the
Shin Byu, or at least could sympathize with those who do; that here, something within each of us is significantly touched, so that this ritual of a
distinct group makes sense.[149]

In a series of lectures published in 1967, Professor Smith has addressed
himself to the question of religious truth.[150] Since he finds that the study of
'religion' is the study of persons, it may not be too surprising that his answer
to the question 'Can religions be true or false?' is 'No'. Religions cannot be
true or false since truth does not reside in 'religions' but in persons, and

ultimately, in God. To begin with, what is commonly understood by the 'religions' are the historical or cumulative traditions. But whether one considers 'Christianity' or 'Buddhism' or 'Hinduism', these 'traditions' are so diverse and voluminous that it is not meaningful to say that they are true or false as entities. This diversity is so overwhelming that time would not permit the study necessary to judge the truth of any one of 'them'.

One small way of calling attention to the historical variety, might be to assert, what I have no hesitation in putting forward, that no man in one lifetime of study could possibly become sufficiently well informed on the history of either the Buddhist or the Hindu communities to be able to say that Buddhism or Hinduism is true, or alternatively, is false, and know what he was saying.[151]

This diversity of religious traditions to which Smith points extends not only into the remote past, but into the indefinite future. 'The future religious history of mankind is open.'[152] Given the nature of historical change, it is simply impossible to say what the 'Hindu' or 'Buddhist' or 'Christian' faith will be tomorrow, or one hundred years hence.

I personally believe that if one is going to talk of religions at all, then one must recognize that every religion is new every morning. Some might wish to exclude their own reified system from this at the price of depersonalizing it; but no one can exclude the Hindu and Buddhist traditions.[153]

More than this, Smith rejects the notion that the truth question resides in the religions since he sees the religions as reifications of personal faith. Hence he has, in *The Meaning and End of Religion*, suggested the abandonment of such terminology since it falsifies what we are really attempting to get at. Since, then, he has rejected 'religion' or the 'religions' as valid objects of inquiry, it is now pointless to ask if they are true. It would indeed be possible for Smith to say: 'If there are no religions, then clearly they cannot be true or false, and the matter is ended'.[154]

However, Smith does not want to ignore the significance of the question that is being asked, even though he does not approve of the form in which it is asked. Ever since the Enlightenment, Westerners have emphasized the rational, the intellectual, the doctrinal. But when one asks the question of religious truth, he is not, at best, asking a theological question. The question of religious truth is a crucial one, but it is necessary to appraise rightly where the locus of truth lies. It lies not in the religions, the systems, the cumulative traditions; it lies in persons.

> We talk blandly of the religion to which he belongs; ought we not rather to concern ourselves with the religion that belongs to him? God is interested in persons, not in types.[155]

Smith is more concerned here with existential truth than with the truth of propositions. The reason is that propositions can exist independently of the experience of persons. He holds that it is the degree of apprehension of what is intended in the cumulative tradition that determines the degree of religious truth.

> No person, admittedly, is religious in a vacuum. He becomes religious by participating in one or other of the historical religious traditions. Yet each man's participation is his own. And religious truth or falsity lies in that participation, rather than having been determined in advance by the institutional pattern.[156]

Hence, when one is asking the question of religious truth, one is asking a question not about religions, but about persons. This means that one's 'Christianity' or 'Hinduism' is not in itself true, but it 'can *become* true, if and as you or I appropriate it to ourselves and interiorize it, insofar as we live it out from day to day'.[157] It is possible to say that one man's 'Christianity' is more true or more false than the 'Christianity' of another person. And, it is possible to say that my 'Christianity' is more true today than it was yesterday. Across traditional lines, it is quite possible to say that a given Muslim's 'Islām' is either more true or more false than a given Christian's 'Chistianity'.

> I think it would be quite impossible to challenge the following contention: that if the terms 'true' and 'false' here have any meaning or relevance, then the concrete, personal religious life of a particular Christian may be more true, and it may be more false, than that of a particular Muslim.[158]

Smith does not completely ignore the question that is usually intended when one asks if a given religion is true, namely, the truth of propositions. But even here he contends that God is primarily concerned with persons. In the context of speaking of the truth of statements, he says: 'Yet I cannot see complications even here. I can see persons even here. And I believe that even God sees persons primarily, even here'.[159] But one may change terms so that truth refers to existential truth without solving this problem. It so happens that Smith's statement 'And I believe that even God sees persons primarily, even here' is a proposition which is either true or false. And, if it is false, that is so much the worse for Smith's position, persons or no persons. However, our concern here is not to enter into a theological critique, but merely to indicate that Smith does address himself to this question, and in so doing enters into the normative level.

We have asked of both Malinowski and Eliade, where we also detected normative overtones, whether it would be possible to use their method for the study of man's religions if it were divorced from their normative positions. In the case of Malinowski we found that this would be possible. In the case of Eliade, we found that without his ontological assumptions his entire method would become merely a means of organization, losing its methodological distinctiveness.

In the case of Wilfred Cantwell Smith, it would seem quite possible to utilize his method without accepting his notion of religious truth. It would be quite possible, for various reasons, to be interested in the faiths of other men, and to attempt to come to what might be a 'personal understanding'.

There are certain limitations to this method, however, which should be pointed out. It is in principle applicable to all persons, past and present to whom we have adequate access. In point of fact, however, most past persons do not offer us such access. Hence the method, which is in principle of universal application, is in practice most useful for living persons who can be engaged in dialogue and discussion.

It might be useful at this point, to notice that while Smith is close to our functional-definitional approach in that he does proceed by defining the categories with which he chooses to work, namely, 'faith' and 'cumulative tradition', there seems to be a basic misunderstanding of the nature of category formation. He feels that 'religion' and the 'religions' are no longer usable since they have taken on the connotation of a reified entity. He would dispose of both. But we have pointed out that all words are ambiguous, and we might at this point notice that the same is true of 'faith'. This term has also been reified, and no less than Paul Tillich has spent considerable time in an attempt to restore what he considers a more adequate meaning to the word. One could conceivably do what Smith wants to do without dispensing with the word 'religion'. Indeed, he seems to find it difficult to dispense with it entirely. One could simply, if he chose, give to 'religion' the functional definition that Smith gives to 'faith', and then be on with it.

The method proposed in this volume is at many points quite close to that of Smith's without the mystifying problem of researching the 'faith' of other men which is scarcely academically accessible.[160] The problem is that the mystery which religion presents is incorporated into one's scholarly work and one takes numerous pages to indicate what would be going on in the mind of a Buddhist boy at the *Shin Byu* rite, and what might come of it in later life, even though such description is pure fancy.

If he becomes, for instance, in modern times, a medical doctor, having gone off to a big city for his education and even perhaps abroad; or if he becomes a modern-type professional social worker, or whatever it may be – *then who can tell* how far the motivation for his career, and the constancy and integrity and devotion with which he pursues it, may be influenced by his experience at this ceremony – or by having grown up in a village and in a home where such a ceremony is traditional.[161]

This is precisely the point: *who can tell*?

But when one is asking the religious question as defined in chapter two of this volume, he is asking a question about persons. Indeed, he is asking the most important question about persons that can be asked historically: what is of ultimate importance to him, or her, or them? And, this question can be asked within the academic arena.

In chapter five we will have cause to return to Smith's method.

D. NORMATIVE UNDERSTANDING:
HENDRIK KRAEMER, HANS KÜNG, AND SARVEPALLI RADHAKRISHNAN

Normative understanding is that level of understanding or knowledge which asks the question of truth. There is a sense in which the functional inquiry is not complete until one has identified true functions, and historical inquiry is incomplete until one's description of the past truly corresponds to that past. But by normative understanding we intend that level of inquiry whose goal is a true account of *reality* rather than merely a true description of accounts about reality. This question is addressed in different ways by theologians and philosophers of religion. However one defines their respective goals and methods, both have frequently addressed themselves to the question of truth. It is not my concern to offer a critical analysis of the most adequate truth system, but merely to illustrate this level of inquiry with a brief description of the approach of three thinkers. We have deliberately chosen to deal with thinkers whose views differ and who fit into diverse traditions. This will serve to indicate that although the normative question can be raised in various ways, its common point is that it always addresses itself to the question of truth. This level is not concerned with the function of a given view of Ultimate Reality, nor with what it means to the believer who holds it, nor merely with an accurate description of the view. Normative understanding asks: 'Is such a view about Ultimate Reality true? Is it worthy of allegiance?'

Hendrik Kraemer

Kraemer holds not only to the validity of a theological starting point in the study of religions, but also to the inevitability of such a point of departure. From its inception, he continues, the 'Science of Religion' operated on the assumption that it was purely objective and scientific. In the minds of such scholars, this distinguished them from dogmatic theologians. But such efforts proceeded only under certain axiomatically accepted presuppositions. Whether it was C. P. Tiele, who assumed that, on the basis of his knowledge of what religion is, he could tabulate a hierarchy of religious truth, or Max Müller whose 'science of religion' included 'comparative theology', the science of religion did not substitute objectivity and science for dogmatics, but merely exchanged one dogmatics for another.

> Intoxicated with this enthusiasm, the pioneers of the Science of Religion overlooked the fact that a different type of dogmatic thinking of various shades and sources – either inimical or friendly towards religion – was being set over against the dogmatic thinking of theology.[162]

Although Joachim Wach held that the science of religion was not normative, and placed the question of truth in suspension, the phenomenological goal of *verstehen* (understanding) was not merely an act of the mind, but involved the total being of a scholar, hence militating against pure objectivity.

> The simple consideration that this kind of *verstehen* as pursued by Phenomenology, cannot be accomplished without real divination and congeniality, without a *verstehende Persönlichkeit* (an understanding mind), shows already that the total being of a scholar, which includes his subjectivity, is called into action. So, just as there always will be a plurality of philosophies of religion, so there will also remain a plurality of phenomenologies.[163]

If a truly scientific approach were possible, one could assume that a consensus would arise. However, this will never happen. Whenever intuition is necessary and one sets up the goal of understanding from within, a purely scientific or objective approach is impossible.

The purely scientific is a fiction, asserts Kraemer. Understanding always involves interpretation, for understanding or comprehending another religion is not merely an intellectual task, but an existential one. It is his belief ın the inevitability of interpretation and the impossibility of an intellectual approach to religion untainted with presuppositions which Kraemer uses to justify the theological starting point. If everyone begins his study with axiomatically accepted presuppositions, then the theologian need not feel that he is at a disadvantage. Moreover, by a full admission of his *a priori* bias, he is not only proceeding as all investigators do, but he is adopting a more scientific approach as well.

> Therefore – and this is a real point we want to make – the theologican can and must do it with a good philosophical conscience, by being faithful to his theological conscience. That is to say, in being a faithful interpreter of God's self-disclosure in Christ, and thereby exercising that interpretation of religion which is implied in his primordial, undemonstrable starting-point. In doing so, and doing it faithfully and methodologically, open to all that he can learn from the Science of Religion, and diligent to the rules of the 'scientific' game, he is not prejudiced, but humanly speaking in the same position as any other honest investigator of religion, whether the latter is conscious of his primordial, undemonstrable starting-point or not. We are, in saying this, not invoking the right of prejudice. On the contrary, by full recognition and avowal of one's bias one is comparatively speaking the better armed against the temptations of prejudice and partiality, to which every scholar without exception is constantly exposed.[164]

Since all scholars have such starting points, the prejudice that historians of religions have had against theologians is misdirected.

If, then, our human condition makes objectivity unattainable, and if the question of truth is inevitably broached, what is Kraemer's norm in his evaluation of religions? Disavowing any make-believe objectivity which comes from concealing from others and even from oneself the presuppositions under which one is operating, Kraemer holds that the Christian has no alternative than to begin with Biblical revelation. Biblical revelation is not the revelation of a set of propositions, but is God's word to man embodied in the person of Christ.

Revelation, of which Christ as a living Person is the final embodiment, is *toto modo* different from Religion. Religion speaks about what man thinks of God. Revelation speaks of what God thinks of man.[165]

Revelation is basically different from intuition and does not arise from human religious consciousness. It originates with God and enters human history in the form of 'sovereign divine words and acts'.[166] Since this revelation is not a body of true propositions, but a divine self-disclosure, the response to revelation is not reason but faith. And, since this is the case, it follows that faith is not an intellectual affirmation to a doctrinal position, but a response to a living person.

The Christian, then, begins with Christ. He cannot undertake his scholarly work detached from this basic relationship implied in the Christian faith.

Under all conditions, in all kinds of work (including this work of interpreting and evaluating non-Christian religions, which calls for a great amount of scholarly work), he remains primarily a disciple, a captive of Jesus Christ, in whom God disclosed Himself, full of grace and truth.[167]

One cannot begin with a general view of religion under which one subsumes Christ. For the Christian, Christ is the norm by which one comes to judge the religions. Kraemer criticized the critics of his 1938 volume *The Christian Message in a Non-Christian World*, who felt that he should have taken a less narrow-minded and more objective standpoint in his approach to other religions.

Their demand was philosophically naive and theologically inadmissable, because the choice is not between 'scientific' objectivity (to use this unsatisfactory word in this context) or alleged theological 'subjectivity' and prejudice, only the first guaranteeing scientific open-mindedness. Rather the crucial question for Christians is: Is Christ the measure of true religion, or is it some general religious *a priori* by which Christ has to be measured? Christians cannot behave as if there is an ultimate religious *a priori*, under which Jesus Christ is subsumed. For them Christ is the religious *a priori*. Non-Christians or non-believers naturally will disavow this, but have to keep in mind that their decision for their religious *a priori* is just as much an act of faith as the Christian's choice for Christ.[168]

It is impossible to demonstrate the truth of any position philosophically since there is no agreed upon criterion for truth. For the Christian, the starting point is the revelation of God in Christ, which is witnessed to in the Bible.

While religions exist in the plural, there is no such thing as religion, which is merely a collective term. The concrete religions always turn out to be different, and hence the legitimate role for the comparative study of religions is contrasting and indicating the peculiar structure and character of the several religions. Each religion is a world in itself with its own center.

What does exist universally is religious consciousness. The theological question includes both this religious consciousness as well as the concrete religions.

The question then runs as follows: Has this religious consciousness, independent of the variegated quality – good and bad – of its fruits and embodiments, anything to do with God of the revelation? Has the God of revelation anything to do with it? If not, why not? If so, why and how? Can one understand religion without taking God into account, that is to say, not as an idea or projection of human needs, but as a reality?[169]

Such a phrasing of the question presupposes that truth is not to be considered as an intellectual construction but as 'the right life-relation of selves, the Divine Self and the human selves'.[170] Therefore, one is not dealing with a question of true or false religions, but of authentic or disoriented religion.

Since the Bible is the record of the words and acts of God, Kraemer attempts to base his theological approach to religions on a sound exegesis, an exegesis which requires that one hold simultaneously that man has lost the *Imago Dei* in the Fall, and that he has also retained it. This is the dialectic which characterizes Kraemer's approach. Both the affirmation and negation must be said in one sentence since anything less would tend to overemphasize one or the other. Kraemer is aware that he has tended to emphasize the negative, but he contends that such an emphasis is due to the general tendencies toward relativism and indifference. At another time and place he might have emphasized the positive side. Ideally the two must be held together in a certain tension.

The mythical story expresses far more effectively than theological or philosophical conceptual languages ever could, that the truth about man is that *he, in religious, moral and psychological respects, i.e. in his total being, finds himself through the Fall in an inescapably dialectical condition,* related to God – separated from Him; sought by God ('Adam, where art thou': God's selfdisclosure to man) and haunted by Him – rebelling against Him and yet groping towards Him. This dialectical condition is the constitutive element of man's religious consciousness.[171] Christian faith, then, is man's appropriate response to God's self-revelation in Christ. The Christian religion is quite another thing. The Christian religion is phenomenal Christianity and is open to the same kind of dialectical 'yes and no' that other religions are.

The Christian religion in its many historical manifestations shows the same disturbing combination of sublime, abject and tolerable elements as the non-Christian religions. Seen from this angle, Christianity as a phenomenon in history has to be considered as *a* form of religion just like the others, although, also like them, it has, of course, its peculiar emphases and concerns. This thesis must constantly be repeated in order to avoid the frequently occuring identification or partial identification of Christianity, one of the religions, with the Revelation of God in Christ.[172]

Kraemer finds the Protestant Reformers, Calvin and Luther, and the twentieth century theologians, Karl Barth and Emil Brunner, closest to the Biblical position. But even here he departs from both Barth and Brunner on the question of general revelation and natural theology. Barth was right in rejecting the notion of general revelation, since all revelation is *special* and ultimately related to Christ. He was also correct in rejecting the notion of natural theology. Both of these doctrines are un-Biblical. But Kraemer cannot understand how Barth, 'the initiator of *dialectical* thinking',[173] could be so undialectical and rationalistic at this point. Brunner is more dialectic, but Kraemer holds that in using the term 'Natural Theology', Brunner departs from the Biblical faith.

It is necessary to admit and to affirm that God's self-disclosure, contained 'in the past, present, and future, through nature, history and conscious-ness',[174] is clearly taught by Paul in Romans 1 and 2. But that man is capable, by reason, of developing a natural theology, is a complete disregard of the biblical doctrine of the Fall. Kraemer objects to using the term 'Special Revelation' for the revelation in Christ since every revelation is special, and all revelation finds its ultimate meaning in Christ. It is true that the religions of men are their responses to the self disclosure of God in nature, history and conscience, but in the light of the Fall, they must be evaluated dialectically. Natural theology presumes that the intellect of man is untouched in the Fall. Revelation is never merely self-discovery.

All religions are huge systems of manifold, partly more or less positive, partly more or less negative, responses to God. The more or less positive ones are always at the same time negative, and the more or less negative ones at the same time positive.[175]

For this reason, to consider the religions as *praeparatio evangelica* or to see Christianity as the 'fulfillment' of other religions is contradictory. As the Indian theologian P. Chenchiah points out, Jesus often kills the aspirations of the religions, or fulfills them in a way contradictory to that expected by the religions.

If it is true that the revelation is 'eine göttliche Aussage über den Menschen' (a divine pronouncement on man) – and it *is* true, if one accepts the revelation as the only criterion for Truth – then to think systematically in terms of 'continuity' as to the relation of the Christian faith to the non-Christian religions is self-defeating and self-contradictory.[176]

One should not attempt to place various modes of revelation in a hierarchy. They all receive their meaning through God's revelation in Christ. This is necessary since the revelation in history and nature both reveals and conceals.

The only thing that should be said is that the central or focal revelation is the revelation of the righteousness of God in Christ, 'the power of God to salvation to every one that believeth', and that the other modes are all of them revelations of God's righteousness in their own specific way, are all related to the central one, and yield their true significance through it, because they all happen through Christ and to Christ.[177]

The only proper approach for the Christian, in the light of Biblical faith, is to examine religions dialectically, recognizing that God has revealed himself to all men, but that in the Fall, man has tended to twist the revelation.

In one Indonesian tribe, a myth which perpetuates the community life of the tribe 'conveys the idea that the life of the world is established in the death and sacrifice of a god...'[178] This is a profound intuition, but it is also perverted into a magical act.

The dialectical condition manifests itself in the fact that this re-enactment of myth is perverted into a magical human act. With all his sacral awe, man behaves as a usurper of God's domain, which is exactly what is meant by 'Original Sin'.[179]

In various religious contexts man has become preoccupied with death and the means to overcome it. The pyramids of Egypt and magical practices among the Chinese are examples. This is both profound and stirring. But it is only a recognition of the 'sting of death' and does not know God since it remains in a 'naturalistic apprehension of life, man and world, in which the cyclical revolution of life and death is an eternal movement'.[180]

When Humanism proceeds with a reverence for 'the divine' as in Socrates, its real center is in *Know thyself*. Hence it actually blocks *authentic* self-knowledge. 'It is constantly said in the Bible, not *Know thyself*, but 'Remember (i.e. bethink thee of) thy Creator', and so come to the right knowledge of self.'[181]

Numerous examples could be given, but in each case there is no intuition of God's holiness. Man appears to want God, but to want Him on his own terms. Even in the so-called parallels of the religions of grace such as Indian bhakti, it is man who takes hold of the idea of divine grace, and so it is less than Biblical faith.

> The famous parallel of the religions of grace confronts us with the fact that man takes hold, of his own accord, of the idea of the divine grace, and leaps on his own account over the reality of his own sin, to assure himself of grace, because he has no idea that he really has to deal with the holy God. His exultation in grace and grace alone is paradoxically an act of self-pardoning. This indulging in divine grace is therefore utterly different from the Biblical religion of grace, because in the latter divine grace has its real meaning in the fact that it is a different way of saying: divine forgiveness of sin, as the root-fact.[182]

The same dialectical manner of dealing with religions must be extended to empirical Christianity. Here there exists the possibility for the greatest fulfillment and also the greatest demonic activity. The Church is the place where God is operating in Christ and through his Holy Spirit. Hence, in spite of the crises, catastrophes and distortions, the Church is still the body of which Christ is the head. But it is this special relationship which makes the Church most susceptible to the demonic. It is because it is the Church that the 'Evil One is more interested and active in tempting the Church in order to destroy it...'.[183]

> It is indispensable to speak here about the Power of Evil in personal terms. He, the *diabolos*, the destroyer, is most vigilant in regard to the Church, the Body of Him 'who came to destroy the works of the devil'.[184]

Christ, then, is the 'Caller in question' of all religion, including the Christian religion.

Now all of this is an attempt at normative understanding because it is an effort to see things as they actually are. It addresses itself to the question of truth.

> This whole book is primarily concerned about the problem of Truth, because it is written as a small contribution to the endeavors in the past present, and future, of explaining what is implied in Jesus' self-evaluation 'I am *the* Truth', and what light is thrown on all other vindications of Truth, scientific and philosophical.[185]

My concern in analyzing normative understanding is not to determine which normative system is true, for that would involve doing theology. What we want to observe is the nature of normative understanding, indicate where it stands in relation to other levels of understanding, and indicate what reductionism might mean in this context. It seems that Kraemer is reductionistic. It might be defensible to argue that in the final analysis all men must raise the normative question, the question, of truth. The validity of such a position could then be discussed on the normative level. But Kraemer has argued that *all* investigation of religion inevitably proceeds on the normative level, and that is quite a different matter. What he has done is to reduce all attempts at accurate description, personal accounts, or functional analyses to theologies based on 'axiomatically accepted presuppositions'. It may well be that the type of 'understanding' which Wach aimed at would require the involvement of the total being of the scholar. Perhaps there is a case to be made for the view that it is the total man who investigates religion and not merely 'an intellect'. But, one might ask whether the 'total man' must always ask the 'total question'. While he may not ultimately do justice to his own totality by not doing so, there are indeed legitimate penultimate questions that can be asked. The total man can ask questions and offer answers on a variety of levels. This is the point of the present chapter. One level is: what truth does this religious expression contain? Another is: what *is* the expression, and what does it mean to the one who uses it?

Hans Küng

That men can be saved even though they find themselves outside the membership of the Catholic Church is no longer in need of debate since it must be affirmed by thinking Catholics everywhere. Such is the position of Hans Küng. Vatican II explicitly affirmed this position in the Constitution on the Church.

Nor is God far distant from those who in shadows and images seek the unknown God; for he gives all men life and breath and all things (cf. Acts 17. 25–28), and as Savior wants all men to be saved (cf. I Tim. 2.4). Those who through no fault of theirs are still ignorant of the Gospel of Christ and of his Church yet sincerely seek God and, with the help of divine grace, strive to do his will as known to them through the voice of their conscience, those men can attain to eternal salvation. Nor does divine providence deny the assistance necessary to salvation to those who, without having attained, through no fault of their own, to an explicit knowledge of God, are striving, not without divine grace, to lead a good life. (Chapter 2. p. 16).[186]

The position that 'outside the Church there is no salvation' has been a dominant theme in Catholic theology. However, it is not to be stressed unduly, since the Council of Trent taught the possibility of baptism by desire, and the Jansenist position that 'outside the Church there is no grace' was condemned by the Church. When Father Feeney of Boston insisted on taking the encyclical *Mystici Corporis* literally in this regard, he was excommunicated. Hence, Father Feeney, who held vigorously that there was no salvation outside the Church, found himself outside the Church.

The Catholic position on this point has been ambiguous, however. While formally holding that 'outside the Church there is no salvation', it has at the same time made provision through baptism by desire and invincible ignorance for the salvation not only of those who have never heard the message of the Church, but those who have heard, but who 'labor under ignorance'.

The origin of this 'ecclesiocentric view' is found in the image of Noah's Ark in I Peter 3:30. Küng points out that although the passage does teach that there is salvation inside the Ark it does not assert the negative position that there is no salvation outside the Ark. For Küng, the text teaches that Christ preached the good news after his death to those 'who formerly did not obey' and hence were not in the Ark. This means that there is salvation outside the Ark but not outside of Christ. Not only in the case of Father Feeney, but throughout the Church's history as well, whenever the negative assertion has been taken literally, it has lead to heresy. When Cyprian held that baptism administered by heretics outside the Church was invalid, his position was rejected by the Church.

Küng feels that it is time for the Church to move from an explicitly 'ecclesiocentric view: outside the Church no salvation' to an explicitly 'theocentric view'. To take the theocentric view means to view mankind as within God's plan of salvation. Küng's conclusion, based on an examination of Scripture, is that all men can be saved. The same God is the God of the Hebrews and of mankind universally.

There is little doubt that the Bible abounds in negative descriptions and condemnations of paganism. But there is another strand which teaches that God is the God of not only his chosen people, but of all men. The prophets criticize not only the 'pagans' but also the people of Israel, with the pagan peoples often 'appearing as those who are fulfilling the divine will.'[187] The priestly tradition begins its discussion with the first man, not with the first Israelite, and interprets the convenant with Noah (which preceeds the covenant with Abraham) as being made with the whole of humanity. Taking the Old Testament as a whole, Küng cannot conclude that ouside of Israel there is only sin and darkness and doom, for God's grace and mercy is at work there as well as within Israel.

Given this whole perspective, it is not astonishing that a whole series of 'holy pagans' is to be found in the Old Testament: Abel, Enoc, Daniel, Noah, Job, Melchizadek, Lot, the Queen of Sheba. There are other pagans too who appear in a friendly light in the Old Testament: the Canaanite woman Shua and Tamar (Gen. 38. 2), Joseph's wife, Asenath (Gen. 41. 50), Pharaoh's daughter (Ex. 2. 5), Moses' father-in-law Jethro (Ex. 18), Rachab (Josh. 2. 1–21), Ruth, Ithra (2 Sam. 17. 25), the sailors in the story of Jonah (Jon. 1. 16) and the varied multitude that was with the people in their journey through the desert (Num. 11. 4). [188]

While Jesus limited his activity to Israel, he rejected all nationalistic feelings of hatred toward Romans and Samaritans, and assumed universalistic titles such as the Son of Man (Daniel 7), Prince of Peace (Zech. 9. 9), and Servant of God (Deutero-Isaiah). He also taught that both the Jews and Gentiles 'would be judged not according to their origin, but solely according to their having practiced or not practiced love towards their neighbor (Matt. 25, 35–46)'.[189]

Paul, who in Romans indicates that all men are under the domination of sin, nevertheless makes several statements of universal intent. He holds that gentiles who have not been given the Law of Moses, nevertheless can possibly keep the law since it is written on their hearts. Paul's basic affirmation is 'Glory and honour and peace for every one who does good, the Jew first and also the Greek. For God shows no partiality'. (Romans 2. 10f). The Fourth Gospel indicates that the Creator is also the Revealer and that the Logos has a universal function: 'the true light that enlightens every man coming into the world' (John 1. 9).

It is clear to Küng that the Bible contains universal testimonies that make it impossible to maintain a purely negativistic approach to the religions of men. Furthermore, the negative statements regarding the sin and darkness of the pagan world are in reference to 'paganism in so far as it sets itself against the saving will of God'[190] and not against the pagan world as such.

All men can be saved! As to what lies outside God and his plan of salvation, this is not the real question at all. If we look at God's plan of salvation, then there is no *extra*, only an *intra*; no outside, only an inside, for 'God desires *all* men to be saved and to come to the knowledge of the truth. For there is *one* God, and there is *one* mediator between God and men, the man Christ Jesus, who gave himself as a ransom for *all*' (I Tim. 2. 4–6).[191]

There is sin, darkness, and confusion in the world religions. However, the religions still proclaim the truth of God in Christ. Traditionally, the Church was the ordinary way of salvation, the extraordinary way referring to those who are saved through implicit faith, baptism by desire, or who because of invincible ignorance are found blameless. For Küng, the world religions are the ordinary way of salvation while the Church is the extraordinary way. God is the Lord of the universal salvation history of mankind as well as the special salvation history of the Church. Every historical situation is included within his grace. The implication is that the world religions are not to be conquered since they are legitimate in God's plan for the salvation of all men.

Since God seriously and effectively wills that *all* men should be saved and that none should be lost unless by his own fault, every man is intended to find his salvation within his own historical condition. 'Within his own historical condition' here means: within his particular individual and social environment, from which he cannot simply escape, and, finally, within the religion imposed on him by society.[192]

Although God does not will every aspect of the world religions, he seriously wills them as 'legitimate religions which have a relative providential right to existence'.[193] Since then, God's will is that the ordinary way of salvation is the world religions in which men are found, it follows that man has both a right and duty to seek God 'within that religion in which the hidden God has already found him'.[194]

This radical universalism of the Christian faith means that all of the world religions are under God's grace and can therefore be a way of salvation. This is not a natural theology as such, but the recognition that God's gracious dealings with men are of universal extent.

What is the truth that the world religions teach? Although not recognizing it as such, they teach the truth of Christ whenever they recognize man's need for salvation, recognize God's graciousness, or heed the message of their prophets. At this point, perhaps Küng should be allowed to speak for himself.

1. Despite their errors, the religions teach the truth of Christ when they recognize *man's need of salvation:* when they discern the loneliness, the helpless and forlorn state of man in this world, his abysmal fear and distress, his evil behaviour and false pride; when they see the cruelty, perdition and nothingness of this world, and the meaning and meaninglessness of man's death; when, because of this, they look for something new and long for transformation, rebirth and redemption for man and his world.

2. Despite their errors, the religions teach the truth of Christ when they recognize *God's graciousness:* when that is, they know that the Godhead, for all its nearness, is far off and hidden, that the divine itself must grant us nearness, presence and accessibility; when they know, then, that man cannot draw near to it by himself relying in his own innocence, but that he needs to be purified and reconciled, that he can only arrive at life through death, that sacrifice and sin-offering are needed for the purging of guilt; more, that man cannot redeem himself, but is dependent on the loving mercy of God.

3. Despite all their errors, the religions are teaching the truth of Christ when they listen to the *voice of their prophets:* when they thus, through their prophets, receive courage and strength for a new break-through into greater truth and deeper knowledge, into a revival and renewal of religion as it has been handed down.[195]

However, the world religions contain error as well as truth. They are in an ambiguous position: 'on the one hand embraced, upheld and penetrated by God's grace, and yet on the other hand held fast in the bonds of man's betrayal and wickedness'.[196] Even a cursory examination of the religions will indicate appalling error and moral weakness. The true nature of man and God are often misunderstood either through 'an abrupt dualistic separation' or through an 'overweening monistic union with him'. In the only reference to a specific religion, Küng writes:

> How often, for instance, in Hinduism is the reality of the free and living God either exaggerated in its transcendence into the impersonal absolute of esoteric philosophers or reduced, in its encounter with man, to the anthropomorphic, materialized object of a ritualistic and magical popular piety! Similar things could be said of the Hindu understanding of sin and redemption, of law and providence...[197]

Nevertheless, these religions should not be considered non-Christian, but rather pre-Christian. Since only the full consciousness of Christ will liberate the truth that the world religions contain within darkness, this must continue to be the Christian mission. But this mission is not to conquer the religions, but to serve them. Küng is proposing a theocentric view rather than an ecclesiocentric view. God is bigger than the Church, and can conquer when the Church does not conquer. The Church should not look forward to a time in which religious pluralism will be eliminated, but to a life of service to the world. The goal of the Church is not to convert all persons to the Church, but to lead them within their own religions to find the truth that God has for them there.

> One way in which the Church exists for the sake of the world religions is that she *knows* what the real situation of the world religions is. This is something that the world religions themselves do not know: whence they come, where they now stand, where they are going, what the ultimate situation is between God and man and wherein lies their own true salvation and damnation.[198]

It is because the Church knows this that she can serve the religions.

It is interesting that the discussion that followed the reading of this and other papers on similar themes at the Conference on 'Christian Revelation and non-Christian Religions', at Bombay in 1964, was whether it was appropriate for Catholics to partake of Hindu *Prasad* in their worship, whether Hindu students in Catholic schools should be encouraged to pray and

worship according to their own faith, and whether it was not a possible im
plication that Catholic professors were responsible for giving Hindu religiou
instruction to Hindus attending Catholic schools.

Hans Küng does not evidence the familiarity with the concrete religion
that Hendrik Kraemer does. Therefore, much of his discussion is on the theo
retical level with little if any attempt to apply his theological norms to specifi
cases of the religions. Nevertheless, Küng is attempting a normative level o
understanding in a general way. We are again not concerned with the validit;
of his norms, but simply with pointing out that he operates on the level o
normative understanding and that his position *could* be applied to specifi
cases of the world religions. With a more complete account of Küng'
position on a host of theological matters it would be possible to ascertain a
what points the religions witness to the truth and at what points they are in
error. Küng's emphasis, contra Kraemer, seems to be on the former since h
is looking to the future and to the service of the world religions in thei
striving for the truth of Christ. Although Kraemer is reductionistic when h
maintains that *all* study of religion is inevitably theological, Küng does no
appear to be so. He consciously states that his solutions to these problems ar
from within an explicitly Christian standpoint, without denying the possibilit;
of other levels of understanding.

> We confess from the very start that we are trying to answer this question
> from the *Christian* standpoint. And no one has a right to describe this, in
> advance, as intolerant and exclusive. It may indeed be described as a
> 'dogmatic' standpoint. But on this, it should simply be said that in thi
> sense the non-Christian religions also proceed from a 'dogmatic' o
> 'absolute' standpoint.[199]

This is true whether one is basing his position on the teaching of the Church o
on a mystical experience of the divine which is found in the thought of Rad
hakrishnan.

Regarding Radhakrishnan, Küng states:

> But when he simplifies this identity to the point of asserting that al
> articulate religious statements, all revelations and confessions of faith
> all authorities and rites are relative, and the *only* thing that has any ultim
> ate validity is that inner spiritual experience of the absolute which appear
> in different forms in all religions and can never be adequately expressed
> then he is taking up a *dogmatic* standpoint. It is only possible to make al

religions equal if the underlying formless, mystical experience is being set up as an *absolute*.[200]

Küng, then, is not proceeding on the level of historical understanding, functional analysis, phenomenological understanding, or personal understanding. His is an attempt at normative understanding because he addresses himself to the question of the truth of world religions. His answer is less dialectic than Kraemer's, but it is equally normative.

Sarvepalli Radhakrishnan

Normative understanding is not limited to Christian theologians, but is the level of understanding attempted by anyone who seeks to determine what is true. The disciplinary label by which one is identified in the scholarly world is not always indicative of the fact that the normative level is being pursued. Sometimes this level is approached under the guide of the 'science of religions', while on other occasions it operates under the disciplinary label of theology or philosophy. Radhakrishnan provides an example from the area of philosophy.

As a philosopher, Radhakrishnan has been honored as the subject of one volume of the Library of Living Philosophers. Many of his works appear to be broadly classed as history of ideas or history of philosophy (Indian philosophy), but often his works intersperse statements of a normative and apologetic nature along with statements which are more characteristically descriptive.

There is another reason for considering Radhakrishnan on the question of normative understanding. Not only does it show that this level is not limited to those who call themselves theologians, but it also indicates that this level of understanding is not limited to those who call themselves Christians. One can raise the normative question in dialectic form as does Hendrik Kraemer, as an extension of salvation history as does Hans Küng, or on the basis of Vedānta as in the case with Radhakrishnan. While Radhakrishnan has written voluminously on Indian thought and on its encounter with Western thought forms, our purposes are served by specific reference to a lecture entitled 'Comparative Religion', delivered at Manchester College, Oxford, in 1929.[201] While it is instructive to note that Radhakrishnan sees the science of 'Comparative Religion' as offering the following conclusions, it is his general approach which is our primary consideration.

As Radhakrishnan sees it, 'Comparative Religion' divests us of exclusivistic views as to the truth of our own position and the error of the religions of others. 'It is the natural tendency of the human mind to suppose that its own god is God of all the earth, while all other gods are "mumbo jumbo" made with human hands.'202

One objection that has been made to the scientific study of religion is that its attitude of detachment and impartiality is a threat to religion itself. Radhakrishnan answers this objection by pointing out that

...truth is higher than any religion and a truly scientific attitude in these matters will ultimately result in gain immeasurably greater than any loss we may incur in the process. At the same time, while we may surrender our exclusive claims, the religion in which we were brought up will still exert a peculiar charm and fascination over us.203

Although Radhakrishnan holds that Comparative Religion is a scientific approach, he also holds that it postulates that all faiths have some value.204 Comparative Religion shows that behind all of the religions there is the same striving, the same intention, and the same faith. This is the *Sanātana Dharma* of which he speaks elsewhere in his works.

I would contend that this position is not arrived at by a 'scientific study' of man's religions. Instead, it is Radhakrishnan's answer to the normative question of the validity of the conflicting truth claims of the religions. Furthermore, the answer is not self-evident, but is a dimension of his *Advaita* philosophy. In raising the normative question I have not attempted to answer the question as to which normative understanding is true. What I am trying to point out here is the level on which normative understanding operates. Therefore, I am not arguing that Radhakrishnan is either correct or mistaken in his normative approach, but that it *is* a normative approach.

It is Radhakrishnan's view that all religions spring from the same source and are all 'engaged in a common effort to build a higher and more stable life"205 All of the various religions are therefore less than Absolute. Religions may take various forms, even though they ultimately point men in the same direction. All of this is brought to light by Comparative Religion.

Behind all the varied expressions, Brahman, Yahveh, Ahuramazda, Allah, there is the same intention, the same striving, the same faith. All religions spring from the sacred soil of the human mind and are quickened by the same spirit. The different systems are tentative adjustments, more or less satisfactory, to spiritual reality. Comparative Religion accounts for their similarities by affirming that the human spirit feels after the same spiritual reality, and is in some manner acted upon by it.[206] When Comparative Religion is used with imagination and sympathy, it will enable men to see the common background of the different religions and will reveal the diversity of human nature. This view is supported by various references from the Vedas and from certain Christian thinkers of the *logos spermatikos* type. Even Max Müller is brought in to support this position. I hold that there is a divine element in every one of the great religions of the world. I consider it blasphemous to call them the work of the devil, when they are the work of God; and I hold that there is nowhere any belief in God except as the result of a divine revelation, the effect of a divine spirit working in man. I could not call myself a Christian if I were to believe otherwise, if I were to force myself against all my deepest instincts to believe that the prayers of Christians were the only prayers that God could understand. All religions are merely stammerings, our own as much as that of the Brahmins. They all have to be translated; and I have no doubt they all will be translated whatever their short-comings may be.[207] One implication of this normative approach is that it is no longer valid to use the distinction of true or false in dealing with religions.[208] 'Generally the distinction between true and false is identical with mine and thine'.[209] Hence Radhakrishnan also rejects the contrast between natural and revealed religion since 'revelation is a universal gift, not a parochial possession'.[210]

It is not particularly fruitful to debate the point as to whether Radhakrishnan's view is what Comparative Religion is, for that would become a matter of functional definition. What is important, however, is to note that this is a normative level of understanding in principle, and it is therefore not verifiable through an examination of historically derived empirical data. Whether religions are partially the result of human sin and the Fall, whether they stem from God's gracious activity in history, or whether they are so many manifestations of man's universal search for God, is a question that is settled on a level other than by an examination of empirical data. The general principles are determined on normative grounds. When they have been clearly decided upon, then which specific religious expressions are valuable or true can only be determined through an examination of the available data. However, an examination of empirical data alone will never indicate whether a religious expression is ordained by God or whether it is a subterfuge for demonic activity.

Whether one's normative level proceeds exclusively or inclusively, then, does not make it less than normative. It might be pointed out that on the normative level, there is no such position as a thoroughly inclusive one.[211] Even the most inclusive position is not able to include the exclusivist position *on its own terms*. The recognition of this is not a judgment in favor of any particular position, but the recognition that all normative positions are somewhat exclusivist, for when one takes a given position he is unable to affirm its opposite.

A final observation must be made regarding the nature of normative understanding. Since we have defined understanding as having taken place when valid knowledge has been obtained, and since, in principle, the normative level of understanding asks the question of metaphysical truth, it follows that in fact, normative understanding is less than understanding unless its normative stance is true. This is not to say anything more than that if valid knowledge is obtained on the normative level, then the position must be a true one. On the level of religio-historical understanding as put forth in chapters two and three, the same point does not apply. The reason for this is that the heuristic device of investigating data on the religio-historical level is not committed to a specific metaphysical position. When the data fails to yield an answer to the heuristic question asked on the historical, or functional, or personal levels, one is obliged to say that he has found no answer to his question. Nothing is lost if nothing is found. Since the level is provisional and heuristic, an answer to the question is not a necessary correlary to asking the question.

On the normative level, however, this is not the case. If one decides to handle the truth question in terms of the dialectic of Kraemer, then it is a foregone conclusion that all religions will be dealt with dialectically. If one intends to see them as all moving in the same basic direction, then it is equally clear that all religions will have to be seen in that light. In principle, the level of normative understanding is legitimate, and is probably the final question that man is capable of asking. But if it is to yield understanding (valid knowledge), in fact as well as in principle, then the normative system which is used to evaluate the truth of other expressions must be true. How one decides the truth of a normative system is another question which stands outside our present deliberations. But in point of fact, normative understanding takes place only when the normative position is the right one, that is, when it is true. And, for Radhakrishnan to answer that no such religious position is true to the exclusion of others hardly settles the matter, since it is itself part of a religious position which is in need of normative justification.

Understanding, then, is complex, and can take place on several levels. One has acquired religio-historical understanding when he has offered an accurate description of the pattern of ultimacy for a person or community, or has accurately described the changing historical dimensions of ultimacy. Functional understanding (psychological or social) occurs when one has described the function or functions of a religious rite, belief, or myth. Personal understanding has taken place when one has described the faith of another person or group in such a way that they can affirm the description. Normative understanding has occurred when one has understood the degree of truth contained in the religious expressions under consideration. This requires that one not only has the necessary empirical data at his disposal, but also that his normative system is true. And, it is difficult to deny, in the light of our analysis of phenomenological understanding, that phenomenological understanding occurs when the data it uses is accurately reported *and* to the extent that the ontological system on which it is based is true.

5

Some Inadequate Categories

Given the task of the historian of religions as defined in the *primary categories* of 'religion' and 'history', certain *subordinate categories* must be ruled as inadequate. These subordinate categories are not inadequate because they are false rather than true, for we have seen that such is not the nature of categories. Categories are inadequate because they are not useful in enabling the scholar to do what he has chosen to do. They are inadequate when they prove to be a barrier to the investigation of human data on the level of his choice. The functional definitions of the primary categories of 'religion' and 'history' as developed in chapters two and three serve to indicate the level on which our investigation of human data would proceed. It now remains to be indicated that there are certain subordinate categories which have had prominent usage and which must now be seen as inadequate for religio-historical study. These categories, therefore, ought to be dropped.

Such inadequate categories to be considered are 'the religions', syncretism, and transhistorical religious structures. But, since Wilfred Cantwell Smith has also proposed that 'religion' is an inadequate category, it is necessary to address ourselves further to the retention of the category of 'religion'.

A. RELIGION: AN ADEQUATE PRIMARY CATEGORY

We have argued that by offering a functional definition of religion as a primary category one indicates the level on which he intends to understand human data. There is no need to avoid the word religion by reason of its ambiguity since that is true of most words. Ambiguity is eliminated by means of a functional definition. Since, however, it has been proposed that the word religion be dropped as a prerequisite to understanding the faiths of men, it is necessary at this point to consider this objection.

Professor Smith chooses to drop the word 'religion' since it is of no concern to the man of faith and since there is nothing which corresponds to 'religion' in the objective world.[1] His view is based on the notion that what we have generally intended by the word 'religion' points to an intensely personal human dimension and can never be separated from the people to whom it refers. Having made the point that 'comparative religions' is the study of persons, and having argued at length that the meaning of religion has gradually become reified and separated from persons, Smith takes the step of rejecting the use of the word as a category: 'religion' is a misleading, confusing, and distorting concept. Having quoted eminent thinkers from various traditions regarding their dissatisfaction with the word 'religion,' Smith concludes:

> I have become strongly convinced that the vitality of personal faith, on the one hand, and, on the other hand (quite separately), progress in understanding – even at the academic level – of the traditions of other people throughout history and throughout the world, are both seriously blocked by our attempt to conceptualize what is involved in each case in terms of (a) religion.[2]

There are two reasons why such a step is unnecessary and unfortunate. The first reason has to do with the nature of functional definitions and verbal ambiguity which has been developed in the present study. One of the alternative words for 'religion' in Smith's study, as we have previously noted, is 'faith'. While Smith's definition of 'faith' certainly sustains his concern for the personal dimension in the study of man's religions, it must be conceded that the word 'faith' has had as many variations in meaning as religion has, and it has also undergone its own reification. 'There are few words in the language of religion which cry for as much semantic purging as the word faith.'[4]

For some, faith refers to a personal relationship of trust. But for others it has been thoroughly intellectualized. And, while Smith may well say 'there is nothing in heaven or on earth that can legitimately be called *the* Christian faith',[5] it must be conceded that there are those believers for whom a distinction between 'my faith' and '*the* Christian faith' does not exist. 'Faith', no less than 'religion', has been reified so as to refer to a system of thought. Paul Tillich and other religious thinkers have attempted to restore a personal dimension to both words. Let it at least be conceded that a variety of meanings, one of which involves reification is not sufficient ground for dispensing with 'religion' without also dropping 'faith'. And, if one can render serviceable the word 'faith' by defining it, one can save the word 'religion' as well. Both 'faith' and 'religion' are ambiguous in common and scholarly usage. But ambiguity is eliminated through a functional definition and not by substituting one ambiguous word for another. Smith has in fact eliminated the ambiguity of 'faith' through a functional definition. But the same can be done for 'religion'.

A second reason for not dispensing with the word religion has to do with the goal of religio-historical understanding. The historian of religions (even as a professor of 'Comparative faith') cannot allow himself to take the side of the opponents of reification. Smith holds that the people who are *truly* religious do not concern themselves with 'religion'.

> I am not saying that the concept of religion is inadequate; rather, so far, that it is inadequate for the man of faith.

> The more direct, immediate, and profound his faith, the more he is concerned with something, or Someone, that far transcends anything that can be denominated as religion. The concept is fundamentally a distraction to his religiousness.[6]

Again, 'No man has seen the point of his own religious tradition for whom the concept religion is an adequate indication of what it is all about'.[7]

Such a judgment is subjective and selective. In fact, such selectivity seems to go against Smith's alleged interest in persons. Even if it is the 'faith' of other men that we want to understand, it must be apparent that there are those for whom 'religion' is a meaningful way of expressing their 'faith'. Do we dismiss Radhakrishnan as one whose faith is less than sensitive because he writes books about 'religion' and is a defender of 'Hinduism'?[8] The presentation of statements by believers from various traditions to the effect that their traditions are not religions leads Smith to the conclusion that for men of 'sensitive faith' such a judgment must hold. But numerous others in fact use such terms. Are they not also to be understood? It may be that the contributors to Kenneth Morgan's books, *Islam the Straight Path, The Path of the Buddha,* and *The Religion of the Hindus* are aware of the Western audience for whom they write, but they use reified concepts with little discomfort.

The important point, if we are to understand other people, is not who originated a term or whether it was first applied by an outsider.[9] If a label is utilized by a believer to refer to his faith, even if that label be 'religion', then it need not and cannot be avoided simply because it *originated* in the mind of an outsider. The fact that some persons find reification unacceptable is not deter-minative in this regard. Indeed, according to Smith's study of reification, the majority of persons from the eighteenth century onward would not qualify as 'men of faith'. At this point the seriousness with which Smith takes persons is placed in question – unless we are to conclude that he means only his kind of persons.

The word 'religion' has indeed been a nebulous term, which, if the scholar is to proceed with clarity, must be given a functional definition prior to his investigation rather than at the end of his study. There is no reason to consider 'religion' an inadequate category so long as it is rendered unambiguous through definition. Such a procedure merely indicates the level on which one intends his study to proceed.

There is, however, something that is often done under the guise of the term 'religion' which is illegitimate for religio-historical study, and that is the histor-ical search for the 'essence' of religion. According to Eliade, phenomenology of religion (the search for structures) seeks to understand the essence of religion. C. J. Bleeker sees this search as the final goal of the historian of religions as well. He concedes that the historian of religions proceeds with a certain notion of what religion is, but that his final goal is to determine the essence of religion.

> The student of the history of religions and of the phenomenology of religion starts his study with an intuitive, hardly formulated, axiomatic notion of what religion is. His ultimate aim is an inclusive formulation of the essence of religion. Such a definition is the crowning of the whole work.[10]

Bleeker considers various attempts to express the essence of religion in the form of a short definition and finds them wanting. An example is his rejection of the key word 'power' as getting to the heart of religion.

> ...'power' in itself is not sufficiently qualified and does not furnish a valid guarantee that it represents the object of genuine religion: besides divine power there is also demonical and satanical power.[11]

In announcing the failure of a host of considered definitions, however, Bleeker does not sufficiently appreciate the circular method that is employed in attempts to determine the 'essence' of religion by an examination of historical data. To criticize a definition of religion, one requires a certain notion of what religion 'really is'. That is, one is laboring under the essential-intuitional approach which is a cryptic way of operating under another definition. To contend that one cannot define what he is examining prior to its examination is contradictory. It is further to be questioned whether such a vague notion will suffice in enabling one to identify that for which he is looking. Such a procedure makes it difficult for fellow scholars to ascertain whether what is being examined is indeed religion, and, therefore, whether the 'resulting' definition is actually its 'essence'.[12]

There is no way for one who proposes to study religion to avoid the methodological necessity of beginning with an explicit functional definition of what is intended by the word, that is, a definition that will enable him to identify the object or level of inquiry. Since the 'essence' finally arrived at is already contained in the original definition (even if implicit and vague), there is no real point in asking the question of 'essence'. The difficulty with most definitions is not that they already imply an 'essence' (here we are dealing with analytic truth which makes the subsequent search only a broadening and deepening of what is already contained in the definition), but that by operating with the essential-intuitional approach, the 'essence' found is equated with ontological truth. By utilizing our definition as a functional one we are operating non-judgmentally in order to understand *whatever* has concerned men ultimately. The concern of Bleeker to distinguish between pure and impure religion is no longer relevant since a functional definition, while allowing us to identify religion from that which is not religion, renders useless the categories of 'pure' and 'impure'.[13] These categories are subtly ontological and suggest a hidden search for true religion, or *truth*.

Furthermore, there is no need for the category 'quasi-religious' which has been applied to nationalism or Marxism. If such are systems incorporating ultimate concerns (and I think that in some cases they are), then they are religious, not quasi-religious. If they do not incorporate ultimate concerns they are not religious at all. In any case the category 'quasi-religious' serves no distinct purpose. Our concern, then, is simply to gain an historical understanding of the religions of men.[14]

Dropping the question of 'essence' does not involve a loss, for such a question encounters insuperable logical problems. The 'essence' of religion usually means what all religious men have in common. But all religious men have in common whatever it is that one decides to use to identify them as 'religious'. That is, we are dealing with analytic and not synthetic truth.

To suggest that what is common to all ultimate concerns involves more than that they concern men ultimately is to raise what is basically a non-religious question. For, in searching for this level of commonness, one is forced to deal with characteristics that, while included in all patterns of ultimate concern, are not equally important to all. This seems to point to the fact that the ultimate concerns and the patterns of ultimacy are not actually the same. To consider something essential to all ultimate concerns which goes beyond the definitional tautology would demand that one insist either that all men are in agreement on the content of their ultimate concerns (an obviously indefensible position), or it would necessitate emphasing universal elements which are central to one religion but peripheral to another. But if religion is seen as ultimate concern, to compare what is in one case ultimate and in another case peripheral is not to compare similarities at all. Hence, in the former alternative one is giving a religious answer which the historical data do not confirm, whereas, in the latter the answer is supported by historical data only because it is no longer religious.

The search for the 'essence' of religion is subtly normative rather than historical-descriptive. It implies that the historical accidents can be forfeited without loss. But the 'essence' that is 'found' as the result of this historical inquiry turns out to be simply another *Anschauung*, historically speaking. The logic fallacy of such a procedure is nowhere more clearly seen than in the attempt of Arnold Toynbee to disengage the essence from the non-essentials in the religions'.[15] According to Toynbee, one of man's perennial problems is self-centeredness, and the historian's method is well suited to correct this. Once one, through studying another culture, has interested himself in other people for their own sake, he will come to see that these other people in their time and place have as much right to consider themselves as the center of the universe as we do. He will also see how little right he has to do so. I will not presently go into detail regarding the extent to which the claim to have found the essence of religion amounts to claiming to occupy a new center of the universe.

When Toynbee talks about the essence and the non-essentials, he has reference to what he calls the 'higher religions', of which there are seven: Hinduism, Theravada, Buddhism, Mahayana Buddhism, Christianity, Judaism, Islam, and Zoroastrianism. But the material included in such categories is not nearly as unified as the labels imply. Hence, when Toynbee points out that all seven religions agree that Ultimate Reality has both an impersonal and and a personal aspect, his point is readily supported. There are some in each 'religion' who have espoused an impersonal ultimate and others who have opted for a decidedly theistic view. By dividing the religious world into these seven categories, one would be more surprised if points of agreement could *not* be found. But this does not touch the question of ascertaining the 'essence' of all religions. Apart from the fact that these categories leave out a large segment of religious men in non-literate cultures, it would be easier to find a commonness *among* 'the religions' than it would be to find it *within* them. It is easier to point out that some 'Hindus' and some 'Christians' affirm a personal dimension to Ultimate Reality than it is to find what is agreed upon by all 'Hindus' – or all 'Christians' for that matter. Mordecai Kaplan has pointed out that there is no distinctly Jewish concept of God. He argues that in this matter the continental divide is Kant, and that post-Kantian 'Jews' and post-Kantian 'Christians' have more in common in their views of God than either of them have with pre-Kantian 'Jews' or 'Christians'. The point is that the varieties of religious expression and ultimate concerns are in such classifications as great within each category as among the categories

Having erred regarding 'the religions', Toynbee continues by making a second methodological mistake. In the 'higher religions', he claims, there are two ingredients: (1) essential counsels and truths, and (2) non-essential practices and propositions. The essential counsels are valid for all time. On the other hand, the great religions have influenced their environments and have been influenced by them in return. These influences have left their marks on the religions in the form of accretions which can be verified by the historian who can trace them back to their origin and show that they were independent of the essential truths and counsels. 'He can show that they have attached themselves to the religion, in the course of its history, as a result of historical accidents'.[16] Toynbee recognizes that the 'accidental accretions' are the price that the essential counsels must pay in order to be communicated to people in a given situation. In Christian language, the price of redemption is incarnation The message is eternal, permanent, and universal, but must be put into terms which are local and temporary. Toynbee would do well to remember this The fact is that the so-called 'essence' is always found in local garb, and Toynbee's list of 'essential counsels' is itself no exception.[17] Toynbee is merely translating what he considers essential from one local garb to another which he feels he can affirm and which he hopes will strike an accord with others a well. But to claim that he has in fact stated the pure essence, apart from historical accidents, is absurd.

The historical method which enables Toynbee to identify the accretions actually turns everything into an accretion. The reason for this is that historical method seeks for antecedents and sources, but not for origins in the strict sense. Apart from what the theologians might say about the beginnings of Christianity, the historian is aware that even the sources of 'essential Christianity' are legitimate objects for historical investigation. When the historian, as historian, speaks of the origin of an idea, he means the source from which it came with reference to the object under consideration, and not an absolute beginning. For the historian the 'beginning' does not esist in principle, but only arises when his historical data runs out and he is unable to pursue the matter any further.[18] Historical method is quite capable, given the appropriate evidence, of showing that Toynbee's 'essence' is, within another frame of reference, an accretion.

But, dropping the historical search for the 'essence' of religion does not necessitate the elimination of the word 'religion'. If we propose to study the religious level of human existence, then we must proceed by rendering that level unambiguous through a functional definition. The word is rendered unambiguous not by an *a priori* examination of instances of 'it' in the essential-intuitional manner, but by indicating what we mean by 'it' so that it can be seen whether the instances being examined are religious. This procedure alone guarantees the right of such 'instances' to be considered together, for it alone guarantees that they will have something in common – in our case ultimacy. Commonness is a prerequisite for comparison .For these reasons the category of religion is both adequate and necessary. If another scholar chooses to proceed under another category, such as 'faith' (Wilfred Cantwell Smith) or 'the sacred' (Mircea Eliade), no logical objection can be raised. They have a right to investigate whatever level of human endeavor or divine activity which they choose. But in the interest of clarity they are required to offer a functional definition at the beginning. Avoidance of the word 'religion' by substituting an equally ambiguous word does not result in clarity. But the use of prior functional definitions will enable one to judge whether various scholars are engaging in similar or identical investigations under diverse terminology, or whether divergent investigations are going on under the guise of a single word religion).

B. THE RELIGIONS: HINDUISM AND BUDDHISM

If one intends to investigate 'religion', then, and defines the word as referrin₁
to what concerns men ultimately (either as individuals or in community)
it becomes necessary to reject as subordinate categories the broad and im
precise designations 'Hinduism', 'Buddhism', 'Judaism', 'Christianity',an(
'Islam'.[19]

An examination of historically oriented works (and this is particularly tru
of introductory handbooks), reveals the fact that the categories of 'the reli
gions' are almost universally accepted and seldom if ever questioned. On
would be astonished to find a history of man's religions which did not assum
that the only available categories for interpreting the data are 'Hinduism'
'Buddhism', 'Judaism', 'Christianity', and 'Islam', to name a few. This wa
pointed out in the case of George Foot Moore. Such a phenomenon indicate
that the essential-intuitional approach not only assumes that one can readil
ascertain what religion is, but it is always found in the form of 'the religions'
and that they are equally identifiable, even though they too are difficult t(
define. And so, Moore indicates that Hinduism is 'a protean phenomenon
Even when such designations are seen as oversimplifications of religiou
diversity, they are still used in lieu of better alternatives.

Given the task of the historian of religions, the use of 'the religions' a
subordinate categories is not only misleading, but creates a situation in whic]
the historian of religions is actually precluded from religio-historical under
standing.

But if, one might object, it is possible to offer a functional definition c
religion, why is it not equally possible to offer a functional definition of 'th
religions'? The answer is that it is quite possible. But we have already define(
our goal as religio-historical understanding, and we have defined religion a
what concerns men ultimately. We have assumed that although definitions d(
not exhaust reality, words must nevertheless be defined in order to indicate t
the reader what is intended by their use. We have done this with our primar
categories: religion and history. One might also urge that anyone who insist
upon using the *subordinate categories* of 'the religions' must, in the interest o
clarity, indicate what is meant by such terms and how they assist in reaching th
goal of religio-historical understanding. It is possible that one might want t(
study 'Judaism' without implying that his study is a religious one, or to conten(

that 'religion' is an inadequate *subordinate category* when 'Judaism' or 'Christianity' is the *primary category*. But if one intends to study 'religion', this term must have a prior definition. It is then incumbent upon the scholar to indicate how the *subordinate category* 'Judaism' or 'Hinduism' assists him in reaching religio-historical understanding. It is our contention that such categories preclude the historian of religions from a religio-historical understanding of whole blocks of human data.

The question of the legitimacy of 'the religions' as categories has also been raised by Wilfred Cantwell Smith. His argument for discarding 'the religions' is two-fold. To begin with, he objects to 'the religions' for the same reason that he wished to drop 'religion'. Such categories involve reification and are not relevant to the insider, the man of faith.

> The first score on which I see the concept of a religion as tending to deceive the observer of a community's religious life is, basically, that the concept is necessarily inadequate for the man who believes and therefore cannot but be misleading for the outsider who does not.[20]

Smith here oversimplifies what is acceptable to the believer as he did in his discussion of religion. It is simply untrue that 'the religions' are unacceptable to *all* believers. 'Christians' are idealized to the extent that only a fraction of those who consider themselves 'Christian' can be included when it is said, 'Christian life is a new life, lived in a supernatural context. To understand Christianity, or to think that one does, is not yet to understand Christians'.[21] Here Smith defines out of consideration all but the 'Christians' he intends to understand. There are those who consider themselves 'Christians' for whom the term 'supernatural' is theoretically unfortunate, and others whose lives are lived as though only the 'natural' exists. One may disagree with such a conception of 'Christianity' normatively, but to begin the descriptive task with such a selective principle creates an insuperable barrier for understanding those whose faith is less 'sensitive'. What is said here for 'Christianity' can also be extended to include those who defend *their* Islam, explain the meaning of *their* Judaism (e.g. Mordecai Kaplan in *Judaism as a Civilization*), commend *their* Buddhism as a solution to the problems of world peace (Sixth Buddhist Council), or offer *their* Hinduism as the national religion of India (Hindu Mahasabha). The use of these terms, reification notwithstanding, must be retained in those cases where to exclude them would mean to modify or ignore the articulation of someone's ultimate concern – even if he happens to live on

this side of the eighteenth century. When religion is defined as ultimate concern, every man (even a reificationist) is a potential believer suitable for study
by the historian of religions.

Smith's second argunent for the rejection of 'the religions' is an historical
one. These categories were applied to impossibly large segments of historical
data before the full force of historical flux had been realized.

If it [a 'religion'] exists in one country (or village), it exists in somewhat
different form in the next. The concepts were formed before the ruthlessness of historical change was recognized, in all its disintegrating sweep.
They have in practice been abandoned as awareness has since grown.
It is time now definitely to reject them theoretically, as inherently inept.[22]

A recognition of the complexity and rapidity of historical change makes
Smith's second argument compelling.

How does such a recognition, however, fit into the approach which proposes
to study religion as ultimate concern? If it is the task of the historian of
religions to study the ultimate concern of men, whatever these concerns
happen to be in differing historical contexts, then it is even more compelling
that he discard 'the religions' as *subordinate categories*. Such categories make
the study neither historical nor religious.[23] A study utilizing 'the religions'
as secondary categories is not historical since 'the religions' are categories
which, rather than growing out of an examination of historical data, are
imposed upon a mass of material prior to its examination. And the use of
'the religions' as secondary categories makes the study not genuinely religious
when the goal is understanding the ultimate concerns of men in their givenness, since it imposes one religion or pattern of ultimate concern upon
another. Hence to proceed under such categories precludes the possibility
that the results will be either authentically historical or genuinely religious.

Offering a definition of 'the religions' is often a search for 'essence' and
ontological truth, as was the search for the 'essence' of religion. Since in
historical study, the search for religious essence is actually analytical-circular
in nature, as we have seen in discussing the 'essence' of religion, to give a
definition of 'the religions' implies having made a decision regarding their
'essence'. Let us see how, in two select cases, the use of such secondary
categories as 'the religions' proves to be a barrier to religio-historical understanding.

'*Hinduism*'

If one defines 'Hinduism' in the manner of a neo-Advaitin such as Radhakrishnan or Vivekananda, he will hold that Brahman is ultimately indescribable and transcends personality. Following Śankara, bhakti movements will be valued but relegated to a lower level of reality. Personal deities such as Kṛṣṇa will be seen at best as Saguṇa Brahman or Iśwara. They will ultimately be a concession to ignorance *(avidyā)*. *Mokṣa* will be seen as transcending all dual conceptions inherent in theistic world views. This is one pattern of ultimate concern. But if one accepts such a view of 'Hinduism', he is in a position of foisting one particular religion upon other particular religions.

How can one adequately deal with the 'Hinduism' of Ram Mohan Roy and Devendranāth Tagore, who were thoroughly theistic, and who rejected a metaphysic based on the ultimate identification of Self and God? How can we honestly come to grips with the devotion to a personal deity found in the hymns of the Ālvārs or Nāyanārs, or how can we understand the views of the Tamil Śaivites, for whom the emancipated soul in becoming 'Śivamaya' does not become Śiva himself nor lose separateness, when we have already accepted the interpretation of another believer? Is it of no consequence to the study of religion that, for Śankara, *bhakti* is at best preliminary to *jñāna* while for the *Nārada Bhakti Sūtras* not only is it not preliminary but it is higher than *jñāna*? In the latter, *bhakti* is no means to an end, but contains its own reward. It may be the case that from the Brahmanical point of view Kṛṣṇa is an *avatār* of Viṣṇu who is a manifestation of Brahman. But in passages of the *Bhagavad Gītā*, Kṛṣṇa absorbs the transpersonal Brahman (XIII, 12–17; XIV, 27). In the latter reference Kṛṣṇa is the foundation of Brahman.

> For I am the foundation of Brahman,
> The immortal and imperishable,
> And of the eternal right,
> And of eternal bliss.[24]

We will not reach religio-historical understanding of the Vṛndāvin Gosvāmins who based their theology on the *Bhāgavata Purāṇa* (not the *Chāndogya Upaniṣad* or the *Vedānta Sūtras*), and who were eager to prove that Kṛṣṇa was not merely an *avatār* of Viṣṇu but full God himself, if we see them through the categories of Śankara. Vivekananda is the final authority for *his* 'Hinduism', but that is the end of it. Each person or community that arises must be seen in the light of his or its own formulations. This is truly to take the believer seriously.

When Smith says that it is the task of comparative religion 'to construct statements about religion that are intelligible within at least two traditions simultaneously',[25] he is contending that the believer is the final authority on his own faith. But it must be emphasized that it is sometimes necessary to bypass one believer in order to understand another. This is the limitation of the witness of the believer – he can never speak authoritatively for the vast bodies of religious data that have in the past been categorized within 'the religions'. A believer or a community of believers can at best speak authoritatively regarding *his* or *their* 'Hinduism'. Hence an historical interpretation of Upaniṣadic faith need not have the *imprimatur* of Radhakrishnan in order to be authentic. With living religions we have a check against subjectivity – the living believer. But in the study of the religions of persons or communities of previous generations we are thrust upon the hard realities of historical data. The living Advaitin is of help in understanding the *Chāndogya Upaniṣad* only to the extent to which his insights square with the hard realities of the text. This is not to devalue the ultimate role of the believer, but to take him seriously. When the believer is taken seriously, it is realized that another believer cannot speak for him in any final sense.

'*Buddhism*'

'Buddhism is another *secondary* or *subordinate category* which proves to be a barrier to religio-historical understanding. One 'Buddhism' (Theravāda) is supposedly a system whereby the world and man are seen in terms of the universal principle of impermanence. The solution to the problem of suffering is self-effort. Even the Buddha can do no more than point the way. This 'Buddhism' disavows any element of grace or divine assistance in man's quest for liberation. But another 'Buddhism' ('Pure Land') as part of the Mahāyāna has a developed ontology and has given a primary place to the grace offered by Amida Buddha. In one form, if a devotee merely utters Amida's name a single time in faith, he will enter the Pure Land or Western Paradise at death. While the Pure Land is theoretically only a position from which Nirvāṇa is more readily attained, for many ordinary people it seems to be their goal. Hence, if 'Buddhism' is considered a something, it is a something that is self-contradictory. Religious change has so altered the Theravāda message that there is no way that one can historically hold that the Pure Land doctrine is merely a variation of the same thing.[26] It is the believer (and not all believers at that) who posits a universal 'Buddhism', and it must be said that the 'Buddhism' of various believers differs considerably.

In addition to these more traditional religious forms, there are modern attempts to relate 'the tradition' to contemporary social, scientific, and political problems. In this endeavor, the problems themselves not infrequently usurp the center of the stage and qualify for ultimacy. When the center of attention has shifted, one often has a different form of religion or ultimacy, not a different form of 'Buddhism'.[27] It is difficult to see how such a category as 'Buddhism' could assist us in understanding what has been and and is of ultimate importance to men. Of course, the term will be important as part of the description of the ultimate concerns of some men. There are, to be sure, some men whose ultimate concern is not liberation, but 'Buddhism'. But the mere use of the word tells us little about one's beliefs. That knowledge is acquired only through historical research.

Hence, the label 'Buddhism' is too broad for the purpose of religio-historical study. One might speak of *Religion in Japanese History*, and include discussions of such movements as Pure Land, Nichiren, and others without necessarily using the larger category 'Buddhism' which might make it difficult to understand the religion of Kobo Daishi.[28] But, to speak of *Buddhism: Its Essence and Development* is,[29] apart from the other merits of the volume, methodologically misleading. Are we to suppose that anyone who takes seriously the multifarious materials that have been considered 'Buddhist' is able to ascertain an 'essence'? The title of Kenneth Morgan's book is less vulnerable at this point – *The Path of the Buddha*.[30] With a few exceptions, Richard Robinson's book – *Early Madhyamika in India and China*[31] is able to discuss the thought of a certain school without the use of the term 'Buddhism' as a category. The simple fact is that such a broad designation is useful only when information is scarce, and it is clear that scholarship in the history of religions has progressed to the point that it is now misleading to continue to use such broad categories.

Problems encountered in an effort to reach a religio-historical understanding of the religion of the Burmese further illustrates our point. Religion in Burma seems to involve what has generally been categorized as 'animism' (in this case *nat* worship) and 'Buddhism'. Scholars have encountered difficulty in indicating which 'system' has taken priority over the lives of the Burmese. Buddhism seems to refer to the Theravāda doctrines contained in the Pāli canon and practiced with various degrees of consistency by members of the Sangha. Although Ray urges that 'Buddhism' has replaced the *nats*, this judgment does not coincide with the empirical realities.[32] Another tempting solution is to suggest that the two systems are so hopelessly intertwined that they form a 'syncretistic religion'.[33] This helps little since it sustains two categories that are inadequate and introduces a third category which depends on the maintenance of the former two. Nor can one continue to distinguish the two 'systems' without finding aspects of each within the same persons and thereby failing to understand the religion of these persons. In place of the study of religion, such a procedure substitutes a desire to study 'systems' which in the form they are contemplated seldom exist. Using the same categories Melford E. Spiro argues for the supremacy of 'Buddhism' over 'animism'.[34]

Winston King's otherwise instructive volumes also perpetuate such categories. In his volume *Buddhism and Christianity*, he is aware of the inadequacy of the term 'Buddhism' to account for the various phenomena which are often so designated.[35] He issues the commonly heard insistence that there is no prayer in Theravāda Buddhism.[36] But he continues by describing types of prayers to *nats* made alongside pagodas and sometimes within the very precincts of the pagoda. He also quotes some 'pagoda prayers' which are seen as a perversion of 'Buddhism' by U Thittila.[37] He says: 'However, even though we utterly cast nat worship out of the fold as completely un-Buddhist, there still remains a more Buddhist type of devotion centering around the pagoda'.[38] The fact is that if we want to understand the religion of the Burmese, these categories must be given up. The 'Buddhism' of which King speaks refers to the faith of the Sangha in some cases, but makes it impossible to understand the religion of the peasants who happen to be a majority of the population of Burma.

In terms of these prevalent categories, the peasant who prays to *nats*, offers prayers at a pagoda, and also offers flowers to a Buddha image is neither an 'animist' nor a 'Buddhist'. An understanding of his religion will only begin when we cease allowing the 'orthodox' to define the categories and to describe what he believes the peasant ought to be doing if he is a 'true' Buddhist. 'Buddhism' is *sufficiently different* for the scholarly member of the Sangha and or the uneducated peasant, that it is no longer a serviceable category. Here as elsewhere we are laboring under categories inappropriate for religio-historical understanding.

This is not to deny that there is material to which these categories have been taken to refer. It is to say that whatever definition one favors, it cannot be useful in the religio-historical understanding of mankind since it leaves out a great many religious persons, and since the data which has been included therein is no unity. A requirement for *subordinate or secondary categories* is that they must help to organize and understand the material relevant to the *primary categories*, in this case 'religion' and 'history'. Since the categories of 'the religions' are not a unity in any historical sense, they are not useful in organizing types of 'religion'. Whatever religious types we ultimately employ will likely all be found in each of 'the religions'. The reason the ecumenical movement has been reasonably successful in uniting denominational groups is not because all the persons involved are religiously unified, that is, they do not have the same ultimate concerns, but because all of the religious differences existed within each of the individual denominations prior to merger. Hence, from the religio-historical point of view, no real religious innovation has taken place because all or most of the religious possibilities were preexistent in the separate groups.

Now the same treatment could be made to show that 'Christianity' and 'Judaism' and 'Islam' are not *religiously* monolithic either. One need only pick the extremes of nineteenth century liberal theology and twentieth century fundamental theology to show that in 'Christianity' there are *radical* religious differences. In the one the goodness of man, the love of God, and the ability of man to live an upright ethical life is coupled with a human Jesus and either the elimination of the supernatural or the elevation of everything to the supernatural and miraculous which is about the same thing. On the other hand one has an emphasis on revelation rather than human discovery, the sinfulness of man, the deity of Christ, and an emphasis on divine grace. In most major Christian denominations, 'Christianity' can mean (phenomenally) anything from belief in the five fundamentals to a humanism which affirms faith in man.

The variety of 'Christianities' is matched by radical religious differences within 'Judaism'. If the Orthodox 'Jew' rests in the authority of the Talmud, keeps a kosher kitchen, honors the Sabbath, and expects a coming Messiah, the statement of the early Reform Movement rejects all of these. Reform

'Jews' explicitly stated that they held to unlimited development and that the Talmud was not a divine authority for them. They neither expected nor did they desire a Messiah to lead them back to a land. For Reform thinkers Judaism was basically a religion with a distinct belief in God coupled with an ethical life. Hence all of the cultural matters which made 'Jews' stand out among their neighbors were considered unessential to Judaism. But Mordecai Kaplan and the Reconstructionists hold that there is no distinctively Jewish concept of God, and they see Judaism as a culture or a civilization. Theirs is an explicitly naturalistic philosophy. These are not accidental differences: each case goes to the heart of the matter. If the Reform members considered themselves Jews, the Orthodox were not at all sure. And, if there were an 'essence' to historical 'Judaism', the community itself would have had less difficulty defining who is a 'Jew'.

Since this fact of radical religious difference is characteristic of the other 'religions' on the descriptive level as well, 'the religions' should be dropped as *secondary categories*. Retaining the terms as part of *description* wherever they appear (more frequently in the modern period), and not imposing them where they do not, would be a step toward religio-historical understanding. But having defined religion as ultimate concern it becomes impossible to understand religions of *all* men by utilizing the *secondary categories* of 'the religions'.

Historians of religions would be much ahead in religio-historical understanding if they would formulate their study according to areas in place of 'the religions'. They could then deal with religion in India, religion in China, Africa, Japan, the Middle East, or America, finding appropriate labels for their subject matter as do other historians.[39] The labels should not be composed *a priori* as is the definition of religion which defines the level of investigation, but should grow out of the material studied in good historical method. The final step would involve not the classification of dissimilar ultimate concerns within the categories of 'the religions', (as has been done in the past), but the development of *types* of ultimate concern which would enable the historian of religions to classify ultimate concerns regardless of their appearance in time and space, within or across the categories of 'the religions.'

Syncretism

Another category which adds little if anything to religio-historical understanding is 'syncretism'. It is nevertheless a *secondary category* which has been used frequently to describe certain manifestations in the history of religions. We have noticed its use in certain attempts to understand the religions of the Burmese. Although seldom defined, the word is usually assumed to be abundantly clear, even though examination of its usage reveals that it is used in various and conflicting ways.

Among those who have studied the history of religions, few have used the term as frequently as Hendrik Kraemer. He has written on this theme at some length as both a theological and a missionary problem.[40] Even in Kraemer's writings, however, the term is used with several meanings, and there are times when he employs the term in a manner which he has elsewhere stated is confusing and misleading. There are, for example, those instances where he states explicitly that syncretism is inevitable, necessary, and universal.

> One could go on enumerating, but these examples may suffice to demonstrate the simple fact that syncretism, cultural and religious, is for many reasons a persistent and universal phenomenon in human history. It cannot but happen, unless peoples live in entire isolation.[41]

In this sense it would be possible, one would think, to agree with Radhakrishnan when he says that Christianity is a syncretistic faith and with Hermann Gunkel whose history of religions approach to the Bible led to the same conclusion.

In another context, Kraemer denies that Christianity and Islam are syncretistic religions and that to so label them is misleading. It is, in his view, the Eastern religions which are by nature syncretistic, and that clearly includes Radhakrishnan himself.[42] Kraemer would contend that while one can, in a certain sense, hold that the Christian scriptures and the *Qur'an* are syncretistic, that this is not the best use of that term. Nevertheless, the confusion in usage remains when he also holds that syncretism is universal and inevitable.

One thing should be abundantly clear. Although the term has been frequently used and although it is assumed to communicate its own meaning, that meaning varies not only from one writer to another, but also within the writings of a single author. Some have apparently sensed this ambiguity when they distinguish between conscious and unconscious syncretism.

> In a certain sense every religion, 'primitive' as well as religions related to a big cultural area or claiming to be world-religions, may be and often are called syncretistic to some degree as a result of their growth through history. In these cases, however, the word has various connotations. It

then means that rites or conceptions of different origin, or of a different degree of affinity, have become incorporated in a given religion and have been adapted to its dominant spirit and concern in such a way that they have become a genuine and accepted part of this religion. This, however, has nothing to do with syncretism as a *conscious,* organizing religious principle, such as we have described in the form of genuine, fullfledged syncretism in the Roman Empire.[43]
This distinction is similar to the one that differentiates syncretism as naive or indiscriminative and intentional or reflective.[44] Such distinctions do not solve the problem of varied usage, however, for in either case the meaning of syncretism is determined by what practices or ideas are synthesized and into what kind of apparent unity they are brought, rather than whether it was a conscious synthesis on the part of the participants.

It is my contention that the concept of syncretism has been used in both an historical and a theological or normative sense. An analysis of these two general uses will show that in the former case the term serves no useful purpose at all. The theological sense is not applicable to the faith of those it is sometimes used to describe, but is in reality a barrier to understanding those religions.

Syncretism as an historical phenomenon

Historical analysis limits itself to an explanation of events, persons, movements or ideas which is on the plane of human endeavor. While it may or may not be theologically true that the source of the *Qur'an* is Allāh, it is not legitimate to make that judgment within the limits of historical knowledge. It has been this concern for historical explanation that has led to the historian's preoccupation with the 'roots' of certain movements, or the 'sources' of man's thought. The historian is led to relate the contents of the *Qur'an* to its Arabian setting, and to attempt to show how the Meccan suras and the Medinan suras exemplify a different emphasis, no matter how theologically disconcerting it may be to some Muslims. Historicism goes so far as to imply that an entity cannot be understood unless its history has been traced, and that the significance of the twentieth century approach to life is not that it is scientific, but that understanding itself has become historical. This type of approach goes some distance in explaining the quest for origins whether it be a search for the Jesus of history, the authentic preaching of the early Christian Church, or he authentic teachings of the Buddha.

But such a concern for 'origins' runs counter to the very method that is employed. Within the historical method there is no real room for a beginning, a first cause. The historian must jump into the stream of history somewhere if he is to study anything. One might begin his religio-historical investigation with Sakyamuni, but that is not to deny the historical legitimacy of another study showing the Brahmanical context that made Sakyamuni's position relevant, or still another study showing the features of the Vedic age which preceeded both. The only limitation placed on the historian's quest is the limits of the information available as one moves into the remote past. However, this is not a logical limitation imposed by method, but a limitation imposed by the availability of data. If and when more material becomes available, the historical method will push the historian back still further in his search for historical antecedents.

If the appeal is made to divine revelation such as in the *Qur'an* or the New Testament, the same search is relevant. Even if the *Qur'an* is held to come from Allāh, it was communicated by men and written in Arabic – an Arabic used and understood by the men of Muhammad's day. It has been this search that has involved historians of religions when they apply their method to the study of the Bible. The result has been an insight into the historical relationship between the ideas and practices of the Old Testament and those of the ancient Near East, and the relationship between the New Testament and the Greco-Roman world. Such endeavors are legitimate historical quests even though they may not have the theological implications that have sometimes been attached to them.

One use of the word 'syncretism' is to describe the historical interrelationship between ideas and movements. In this sense syncretism is universal and inevitable and is merely a term used to describe a dictum of historical knowledge–any subject fitting for historical research has historical antecedents.

> Commercial intercourse, political events, the extension of power from a certain centre, often shows such spiritual, religious or cultural encounters and struggles as a mostly unintended consequence. We see, therefore, in the history of mankind many samples and varieties of syncretism. Everywhere, where genuine 'culture-contact' takes place, it appears as an inevitable effect.[45]

It is this method of history which led Hermann Gunkel to say that Christianity is a syncretistic religion. For Gunkel, extraneous elements did not wait until the fifth century to enter the church, but were detectable in the Apostolic age itself. Following an historical method, he located elements in early Christianity that were found in other contexts in the Greco-Roman world and concluded that indeed Christianity is 'a syncretistic religion'. This same observation lends some point to Radhakrishnan's judgment that 'Christianity is a syncretistic faith, a blend of various earlier creeds...'.[46]

Now, if it is true that such borrowing, blending, and influencing on the plane of history is part of the whole historical process and is both inevitable and universal, then no real purpose is served by applying the term syncretism to such a phenomenon. Historically speaking, to say that 'Christianity' or the 'mystery religions' or 'Hinduism' are syncretistic is not to say anything that distinguishes them from anything else and is merely equivalent to admitting that each has a history and can be studied historically. Although Kraemer himself calls this historical phenomenon syncretism, on other occasions he seems to say that this meaning is inadequate.

> The smell of the earth, the brightness of the sky, the natural and spiritual atmosphere, which in the course of ages wrought the soul of a people, have to manifest themselves in the kind of Christianity that grows there. This is far from being syncretism in the technical sense in which it is currently used, but it is a certain kind of coalescence, of symbiosis without losing identity.[47]

I propose, however, that the term syncretism be dropped as a designation of a historical phenomenon. Since in this sense it applies equally well to all religious expressions, to use it to describe a particular expression tells us nothing specific.

Syncretism as a theological phenomenon

When we turn from the meaning of syncretism as a historical phenomenon to what syncretism might mean theologically, we find a certain ambiguity as well. To distinguish between a syncretism that is reflective and conscious and one that is spontaneous may be interesting but it is not a significant logical distinction. Here we are interested in that to which the term applies, whether that something occurs consciously, unconsciously or both.

We shall begin by pointing out that merely to define syncretism as the uniting of religious elements of different origin, or merely as the 'fusion of various beliefs and practices',[48] is too general to avoid the application of the concept to any religious expression. The origin of the elements to be united is not of prime import, and that various beliefs and practices are fused says nothing that would distinguish one movement from another.

Usually, when the concept is applied, it connotes an element of religious conflict or inconsistency. Care must be taken, however, lest the term be used in a manner which is meaningless. To say that syncretism is what takes place when one brings two conflicting ideas or practices and unites them into a harmonious whole is to say nothing coherent. If the two original ideas or practices are in conflict, then they cannot, without modification, produce a harmonious unity. If a harmony is produced, then it follows that either the two original elements were only apparently in conflict, or that changes have been effected so that it is not actually the two conflicting elements which produce the harmony but a modification of those elements which produces elements no longer in conflict. To say that two genuinely conflicting concepts were harmonized is a contradiction.

When elements which have come from differing sources are united into a harmonious unit then the term synthesis might be used to describe the phenomenon. This term indicates the unity achieved without implying the logically impossible statement that the harmony is produced by the union of two contradictory practices or ideas.

What, then, can be intended by the concept 'syncretism'? This term is to be reserved for cases where two conflicting ideas or practices are brought together and are retained without the benefit of consistency. Syncretism occurs only when the result is not a harmonious unity. Kraemer expresses this view in the following manner:

> It is in these circles taken in the sense of a systematic attempt to combine, blend and reconcile inharmonious, even often conflicting, religious elements into a new, so-called synthesis.[49]

This same idea is found when Hocking mentions syncretism as the view whereby one brings together elements from various sources into a whole 'devoid of any principle of coherence'.[50] The same essential lack of unification in syncretism is implicit in H. R. Mackintosh's definition. 'To be strict, syncretism is only present when elements derived from various religions are admitted on equal terms...'[51] Here various elements stand side by side without any attempt to reconcile or give priority to either one.

If, on the other hand, a unity is produced by modifying one's religious complex so that the previously extraneous element is comfortable in that context, then one is referring to what Hocking calls 'reconception'.

Either that good thing you have found belongs uniquely to the religious organism from which it came – in which case you must adopt *that* unity – or it belongs to *yours* – in which case you must *reconceive* the essence of your own faith, to include that new element. You cannot live religiously within a divided house, or a house whose roof covers only part of its floor area![52]

From a theological point of view, reconception may be as unhappy a situation as syncretism, but the two are not the same. In reconception, the result is a unity which has been effected through a modification of the very heart of a religion. This concept, of course, can only be used when one defines the 'essence' of his religion theologically. The attempt to arrive at the 'essence' of a religion by examining its numerous historical manifestations has been shown to be unsuccessful. Syncretism, however, merely retains the conflicting elements without having successfully reconciled them.

The pejorative connotation attached to the term now becomes partially understandable. What could be objectionable in synthesizing religious elements which are not in conflict? It is the willingness to maintain contradictory elements side by side that has been objectionable.

A barrier to religio-historical understanding

The word syncretism is usually not used by a believer to describe his own religion. One of the most common uses of the term in the history of religions is to describe certain Eastern religious expressions. 'Ryobu Shinto' is described as syncretistic,[53] so is the philosophy of Śankara, or the Chinese attitude which enables one to be simultaneously a 'Buddhist', 'Confucianist', or 'Taoist'.

In the grand Mahayanist and Hindu philosophies of religion, for instance, elaborated in Japan in Ryobu-Shinto or in India by Shankara, every stage and expression of religion, from the 'highest' to the 'basest' gets, on this basis, full recognition and justification as to its necessary and relative value. On this syncretistic approach, the claim of absolute tolerance, the pride of all genuinely eastern spirituality depends. Radhakrishnan is, as we have seen, a modernized but essentially unchanged defender of this syncretistic philosophy.[54]

It seems to be implied that in each case the Eastern religious expressions have brought together elements that are conflicting and illegitimate. This is never the religious attitude of those involved, however. They sense no such logical problem. The failure to find a recognition of inconsistency where it might be expected has been problematic for Western scholars.

In the thought of Śankara, for example, there are both levels of being and stages of experience. What is true of one level is not necessarily true of another level. All distinctions, including logical ones, are part of the phenomenal world of appearance. The world of appearance, however, is māyā, that is, illusory from the vantage point of indescribable and indifferentiated Nirguṇa Brahman. The phenomenal world is valid on its own level, but it can be transcended.

So long as the right knowledge of the Brahman as the only reality does not dawn, the world appearance runs on in an orderly manner uncontradicted by the accumulated experience of all men, and as such it must be held to be true. It is only because there comes such a stage in which the world appearance ceases to manifest itself that we have to say from the ultimate and absolute point of view the world appearance is false and unreal.[55]

From the standpoint of Brahman, then, all distinctions of the phenomenal world are obliterated, including ideas and practices that are contradictory on the lower level of being. There is no uncomfortable sense of living with conflict in Śankara's total system. The conflict exists for those who reject the notion of levels of being and who deny the ultimate reality of Nirguṇa Brahman.

Another supposed illustration of syncretism is a Chinese expression.

One of the best-known features of Chinese universalism is that the three religions – Confucianism, Buddhism and Taoism – are virtually treated as one. The religious allegiance of the average man is not related to one of the three religions. He does not belong to a confession or creed. He participates unconcerned as to any apparent lack of consistency, alternatively in Buddhist, Taoist or Confucian rites. He is, by nature, a religious pragmatist.[56]

The important point here is noticed by Kraemer himself. To the Chinese believer there was no inconsistency in such a religious practice for they were treated virtually as one. The reason for this is that there was an over-arching religious attitude which made it possible to incorporate all such practices and beliefs as seemed useful. Kraemer says that the Chinese was in this case a pragmatist by nature. If that be true, then that was his religious attitude, and it was hardly inconsistent to act in the described manner. It is the outsider who does not share such an attitude who fails to recognize its significance. It is also the outsider who uses the word 'syncretism' to describe the phenomenon.

'Ryobu-Shinto' is often given as a good example of syncretism. Here the 'Shinto' Kami and the 'Buddhist' Bodhisattvas are identified and the two religious expressions are merged.

> A really gigantic and systematic attempt towards religious syncretism is Ryobu-Shinto (bi-lateral Shinto). In it Buddhism and Shinto have thoroughly amalgamated on the basis of naturalistic kinship. The great leader in this enterprise of religious amalgamation has been Kobo Daishi, the founder of Shingon.[57]

Here again, however, Kraemer recognizes a basic kinship. This system conceives of Ultimate Reality, or the unobservable source of all existent things, as the cosmic Buddha Maha-Vairochana or Dai Nichi. The universe is the body of Dai Nichi.

> In this manifestation of the Great Life of the Universe on the side of the observable events of experience, the *kami* of the Shinto pantheon appear as the avatars of the divine beings of Buddhism and thus these two faiths are in essence one and the same.[58]

In this system, every 'Shinto' god or goddess becomes a manifestation of the special 'Buddhist' divinity. Hence, Amaterasu-Omikami becomes a particular manifestation of Maha-Vairochana or Dai Nichi.

That some were opposed to Ryobu-Shinto and that others made attempts to eliminate those aspects which were foreign, is no refutation of the unity here expressed, but merely underlines the well-known fact that the terms 'Hinduism', 'Buddhism', 'Christianity', or 'Shinto' do not correspond to a clear and always consistent system of practices and ideas. 'Every faith appears in a variety of forms'.[59] Anesaki points out: 'Now this Double Aspect Shinto was an expression of the compromising attitude so characteristic of the Japanese mind'.[60] Of utmost importance here is that those involved did not look on their amalgamation as involving opposing or conflicting positions. Rather it was a unification that appeared to those involved to be quite legitimate and natural.

Syncretism, then, is irrelevant to those who are inside the so-called 'syncretistic faiths'. 'For those naturalistic religions, which are by nature syncretistic, syncretism is no problem at all. They cannot see it.'[61] If, then, one aims at religio-historical understanding of such faiths, the category is misleading since it does not authentically represent the believer.

Syncretism and the encounter of religions

Kraemer labels most Eastern religions as expressions of religious syncretism. Mahāyāna Buddhism, Advaita Vedānta, Chinese religions in general, Ryobu-Shinto, and the so-called primitive faith encountered in Java, are all syncretistic because they are basically naturalistic (naturalistic-cosmic or naturalistic-monistic).[62] It has already been observed that the insiders in the above cases sense no conflict in their approach. 'In view of the fundamental nature and structure of these religions it is nothing capricious or unprincipled; it is consistency itself. It would be abnormal if this were not so.'[63] The term serves no real purpose *within* the value system of these religions, but reflects instead the value system of the one who uses it. Such an observation is basic to understanding what is involved when the concept of syncretism is used.

We have argued that the only meaningful use of the term syncretism is to describe a situation in which conflicting ideas or practices are brought together into a new complex which is devoid of coherence. But the religious complexes represented by the above illustrations of 'syncretism' are not devoid of coherence to the believers. The term syncretism most clearly denotes not only a lack of coherence in the new pattern of ideas and practices, but also the distinction between the man of faith or insider, and the outsider or observing scholar.

It is no secret that syncretism carries a pejorative connotation.

The scholars intended their statements to be taken objectively and scientifically, but they allowed subjective overtones to creep in. This is well seen in the concept of 'syncretism' which has a deprecatory connotation. If a religion is said to be 'syncretistic', it is held to be *ipso facto* inferior.[64]

This pejorative connotation is readily understandable when it is realized that the concept not only implies a contradiction, but that it is applied from outside the circle of a given faith. The concept of syncretism not only describes the encounter of religions, but *is itself a part of that encounter*. Syncretism is a concept applied to a religion by those who stand outside its circle of faith and hence fail to see or to experience its inner unity. Hence, Kraemer can say that Śankara's philosophy is syncretistic and Radhakrishnan can hurl the same level at 'Christianity'.

Since syncretism in its historical sense is universally applicable and since in its theological sense it is a barrier to authentic religio-historical understanding, its use in religio-historical inquiry should be abandoned.

C. TRANSHISTORICAL RELIGIOUS STRUCTURES

It is not our desire to say that the search for transhistorical religious structures and archetypes which has characterized some forms of phenomenology of religions is illegitimate. Any method which is clearly defined and adequately supported is legitimate. And, the fact that a method may have been poorly defined and inadequately supported in the past is not sufficient ground for saying that it is *inherently* illegitimate.

Nevertheless, we have found that the phenomenological search for structures is ahistorical. The structures and archetypes do not become fully embodied in any historical moment, and it does not matter whether the persons involved have any awareness of the structures in which they participate.

The search for structures may be a legitimate inquiry, but it is not an historical one, and when it enters historical study under the guise of offering the 'religious dimension' of the data, it does violence to authentic historical investigation. Phenomenological structures are not historically falsifiable, and their method of verification is therefore more akin to theological verification than to historical verification. This has been the weakness of the phenomenological method. It has posed as being empirically oriented by offering historical data in support of its proposals. But if the structures found are not historically falsifiable, then they are not historically verifiable. That they are not historically falsifiable is clear from the nature of the trans-conscious, and from the possibility of 'cryptic hierophanies'. Anything that might otherwise be taken as possibly falsifying a religious structure can be considered cryptic. Hence these hierophanies which are clear illuminate those which are not *clear*. But the latter are still 'hierophanies' although they are 'cryptic'. Such a method takes care of any possible conflicting data *a priori*.

When Hendrik Kraemer holds that religion is human sin, there is no *historical* way of falsifying such a theological assertion. For, we are are not working on the historical level here. Regardless of how virtuous actions might *appear* to be, it is always possible that man's sin goes so deep that he is guilty of a self-deceptive use of virtue as a means of self-righteousness. Hence the issue must be settled theologically. The theological and normative probe to a level which the historical cannot. The same is true of Hans Küng's theological position. If he wants to include in God's revelation those who deny the existence of a Supreme Being (The Theravādins), there is little force in pointing out that such persons deny all permanence, that such a denial includes God, and that it is a strange revelation which reveals God by denying his existence. For, no matter how much human sin attempts to cloud the revelation, God is nevertheless there, graciously revealing himself. One might point out that it is merely a repeat of including people in the divine plan 'over their heads', but that is a logical point and not an historical one.

Phenomenology, in the Eliadian style, is like this. It is not historically falsifiable. Since it is an ahistorical approach, however legitimate that might be in itself, when it enters into historical deliberation it becomes a barrier to the attainment of authentic religio-historical understanding. Whether or not it is legitimate to see fertility implications in pearl wearing when such thoughts are not in the mind of the wearer is one question. But how an observation of the way in which a given moment fits into *transhistorical* religious structures, could possibly further historical knowledge is yet another question. Such considerations can only hinder the religio-historical question and its answer.

Now there may be numerous other categories which we are presently using which will be shown to be as inadequate as some of those which we have discussed. One might hope that they will be pointed out in time so that they too be avoided. One might also hope that as we proceed to study the history of religions, new and useful secondary categories will present themselves. But this approach is new, and is not yet in a position to offer a full set of secondary categories.

It may be relevant at this point to counter the probable response to all this. It may sound good, but it is easy to refute the old. It is always more difficult to offer something that is equal or better. We have proposed in this study what the history of religions might be. But to ask what one should use as secondary categories if we dispense with such inadequate categories as 'the religions', syncretism, or transhistorical religious structures, is a non-historical request. Historical categories must come from an examination of human data in a specific time and definite geographical location. To criticize one set of secondary categories because they threaten the authentically historical nature of the study and then to concede the need for another set of equally broad categories is hardly a significant solution. Primary categories must be given in advance of the study so that the level of investigation is clearly defined. Hence we have offered functional definitions of 'religion' and 'history'. Secondary categories depend not only upon their relation to the primary categories but also on their usefulness in understanding the religous dimension of historical data. Hence they cannot be given in advance of the particular data being understood in a religio-historical manner. Perhaps in time such a set *(or sets)* of secondary categories will present themselves to us. They are not presently on the horizon. But that is no reason for utilizing secondary categories which have been shown to be of no use in describing human data from the standpoint of the primary categories defined. Legitimacy must be accorded any secondary category which furthers religio-historical understanding. Secondary categories which hinder such understanding are to be avoided.

Notes and References

NOTES TO 'THE NATURE OF CATEGORY FORMATION'

1. Herbert Spiegelberg, *The Phenomenological Movement. A Historical Introduction*, 2 vols. (The Hague: Martinus Nijhoff, 1960).
   Spiegelberg finds it unnecessary to include a discussion of the application of phenomenological method to the study of religion.
2. Louis Henry Jordan, *Comparative Religion. Its Genesis and Growth* (Edinburgh: T&T Clark, 1905).
3. Mircea Eliade, 'The History of Religions in Retrospect: 1912 and After', *The Journal of Bible and Religion*, 31 (1963), pp. 98–107. Reprinted in *The Quest: History and Meaning in Religion* (Chicago: University of Chicago Press, 1969), pp. 12–36.
4. By an ambiguous word we mean a word which has more than one meaning.
5. Richard Robinson, *Definition* (Oxford: Oxford University Press, 1950), p. 7.
6. Mircea Eliade, *The Quest*, p. 35.
7. The ontological status of the 'Sacred' in the thought of Mircea Eliade will be considered in a later chapter.
8. I am not familiar with any historians of religions who have explicitly accepted this method in the light of this metaphysical baggage.
9. Erwin Ramsdell Goodenough, 'A Historian of Religion Tries to Define Religion', *Zygon: A Journal of Religion and Science*, Vol. 2, No. 1 (1967), pp. 7–22.
10. *History of Religions*, 2 vols. (New York: Charles Scribner's Sons, 1913 & 1919).
11. *Ibid.*, I, Preface, v.
12. *Patterns in Comparative Religion* (Cleveland: The World Publishing Company, 1963), p. xiii.
13. *Ibid.*, p. xiv.
14. *Ibid.*
15. *Ibid.*
16. *Ibid.*, p. xvi.
17. *The Sacred Bridge* (Leiden: E. J. Brill, 1963), p. 39.
18. *Ibid.*, p. 42.
19. *Ibid.*
20. *Ibid.*, pp. 43–44.
21. *Ibid.*, p. 44.
22. *Ibid.*, p. 45.

23. *Ibid.*, p. 51.
24. *Ibid.*, p. 36. *(Emphasis mine)*.
25. A. Eustace Haydon, 'History of Religions', *Religious Thought in the Last Quarter-Century*, ed. G. B. Smith,(Chicago: University of Chicago Press, 1927), pp. 163–164. *(Emphasis mine)*.
26. Philip Ashby, 'The History of Religions', *Religion*, ed. Paul Ramsey (Englewood Cliffs: Prentice-Hall, 1965), p. 5.
27. Leslie A. White, 'On the Concept of Culture', *Theory in Anthropology: A Sourcebook*, ed Robert A. Manners and David Kaplan (Chicago: Aldine Publishing Company, 1968), p. 17.
28. Robinson, *loc. cit.*, pp. 152–189.
29. *Ibid.*, p. 35.
30. Hans L. Zetterberg, *On Theory and Verification in Sociology*, third edition (Totowa, N. J.: The Bedminster Press, 1966), p. 40.
31. Robinson, *loc. cit.*, p. 60.
32. *Ibid.*, p. 66.
33. Leslie A. White, *loc. cit.*, p. 17.
34. Robinson, *loc. cit.*, p. 47.
35. *Ibid.*, p. 46.
36. *Ibid.*, p. 42.
37. *Ibid.*, p. 50.
38. *Ibid.*
39. *Ibid.*, p. 28.
40. *Ibid.*, p. 39.
41. Morton Smith, 'Historical Method in the Study of Religion', *On Method in the History of Religions*, Beiheft 8 of *History and Theory*, ed. James Helfer (Middletown: Wesleyan University Press, 1968).
42. *Ibid.*, p. 8.
43. 'When the notion of definition was invented by Socrates and Plato, only 'real definition' was thought of. That is, it was always *res* or things that required definition, never *nomina* or words or concepts. Definition was in fact, according to Plato, the end of the process of getting to know the most real things there are, which he called Forms or Ideas. Thus a correct statement of the definition of the Good would be an expression of the most important kind of knowledge or insight a man could possibly have... The habit of regarding definition as primarily or exclusively about things has been common ever since.' Robinson, *loc. cit.*, pp. 7–8.
44. I have previously suggested the same thing. 'Dropping the question of essence does not involve a loss, for such a question involves insuperable logical problems. The essence of religion could only mean what all religions have in common, but all religious men have in common whatever it is that one decides to use to identify them as "religious".' Robert D. Baird, 'Interpretative Categories and the History of Religions', *On Method and the History of Religions*, p. 25. Also, cf. Chapter 5.
45. Robinson, *loc. cit.*, p. 155.

46. *Ibid.*, p. 153.
47. There is good reason for dropping the designation 'real definition'. 'I propose then that by "definition" we always mean a process concerning symbols, a process either of equating two symbols or of reporting or proposing a meaning for a symbol; and that we never use "definition" as a name for a process that is not about symbols, because in that usage it is ambiguous and should be replaced by more specific terms.' *Ibid.*, p. 191.
48. *The Phenomenology of Religion* (Philadelphia: Westminster Press, 1963), p. 3.
49. *Ibid.*
50. Robinson, *loc. cit.*, pp. 165–166.
51. Jurji, *loc. cit.*, p. 3.
52. *Ibid.*, p. 4.
53. *Ibid.*
54. Bleeker, *loc. cit.*, p. 51.
55. I will return to this definition in chapter two.
56. Wilfred Cantwell Smith, *The Meaning and End of Religion* (New York: The Macmillan Company, 1962), pp. 48–49.
57. 'Interpretative Categories and the History of Religions', *loc. cit.*, pp. 19–20. Also, cf. Chapter 5.
58. 'Normative Elements in Eliade's Phenomenology of Symbolism', *Union Seminary Quarterly Review*, Vol. XXV, No. 4 (1970), pp. 505–516. Also, cf. Chapter 4.

NOTES TO 'THE CATEGORY OF RELIGION'

1. In chapter III, I will raise the question as to whether this choice makes the study relative to the investigator or whether it makes the answer relative to the question.
2. Such should not be taken to mean that this is a worthy goal for life itself. That would not be a statement of a methodology for the history of religions, but rather a proposal for religious commitment. The present writer would be quick to admit that as the latter this substitutes a penultimate for an ultimate, and is idolatrous. But that is not the point. However penultimate scholarly study might be in terms of an adequate theological perspective, it is still necessary to indicate the goal or end of this penultimate endeavor. Some penultimate endeavors are worth doing too, even though they are not ultimate.
3. Paul Tillich, *Theology of Culture* (New York: Oxford University Press, 1959), pp. 7–8.
4. William A. Christian, *Meaning and Truth in Religion* (Princeton: Princeton University Press, 1964), p. 60.
5. *Ibid.*, p. 61.
6. That Eliade has the ontological reference in mind is clear from a careful examination of his work. This is argued in the author's 'Normative Elements in Eliade's Phenomenology of Symbolism'. It is also discussed in chapter IV.
7. Paul Tillich, *loc. cit.*, p. 3.
8. Mircea Eliade, 'History of Religions and a New Humanism', *History of Religions*, 1 (1961): pp. 1–8. It was reprinted in *The Quest: History and Meaning in Religion* (Chicago: University of Chicago Press, 1969), pp. 1–11.

9. I will argue this at more length in chapter V.
10. Wilfred Cantwell Smith, *The Meaning and End of Religion*, p. 176.
11. Either the affirmation or negation of this assertion is normative and not methodological.
12. Mircea Eliade, *Patterns in Comparative Religion*, pp. 11–12.
13. 'Cultural Fashions and the History of Religions' *The History of Religions: Essays on the Problem of Understanding* (Chicago: University of Chicago Press, 1967), p. 23.
14. 'Introduction', *On Method in the History of Religions*, edited by James S. Helfer Beiheft 8 of *History and Theory* (Wesleyan University Press, 1968), p. 3.
15. *Ibid.*, p. 1.

NOTES TO 'THE CATEGORY OF HISTORY'

1. Joseph M. Kitagawa, 'The History of Religions in America', *History of Religions: Essays in Methodology*, ed. Mircea Eliade and Joseph M. Kitagawa (Chicago: University of Chicago Press, 1959), p. 15.
2. *Ibid.*
3. *Ibid.*
4. *Ibid.*, p. 19.
5. *Ibid.*, p. 14.
6. Sociology of religion and psychology of religion must be considered methods themselves because they do not merely address themselves to a distinct body of data.
7. *Shamanism: Archaic Techniques of Ecstasy*, trans. Willard R. Trask (New York: Pantheon Books, 1964).
8. *Ibid.*, p. xi.
9. *Ibid.*, p. xvii.
10. *Ibid.*, p. xiii.
11. *Ibid.*
12. *Ibid.*, p. xii.
13. *Ibid.*
14. W. H. Walsh, *Philosophy of History: An Introduction* (New York: Harper & Row, 1960), p. 30.
15. Benedetto Croce, 'History and Chronicle', *The Philosophy of History in Our Time*, ed Hans Meyerhoff (Garden City: Doubleday & Company, Inc., 1959), pp. 44 ff.
16. R. G. Collingwood, *The Idea of History* (New York: Oxford University University Press, 1956). Cf. also Sidney Mead, 'Church History Explained', *Church History*, 32:1 p. 21.
17. G. J. Renier, *History, Its Purpose and Method* (New York: Harper & Row, 1956), p. 11
18. Herbert Butterfield, 'Moral Judgments in History', Hans Meyerhoff, *loc. cit.*, p. 244
19. Kitagawa, *loc. cit.*, p. 26.
20. I, 23–24. Robert Ernest Hume, *The Thirteen Principal Upanishads* (Madras: Oxford University Press, 1949), p. 345.
21. Maurice Mandelbaum, *The Problem of Historical Knowledge* (New York: Liveright Publishing Corporation, 1938), p. 19.

2. *Ibid.*, p. 20.

3. E. H. Carr, *What is History?* (New York: Alfred A. Knopf, 1964). p. 24.

4. Fritz Medicus, 'On the Objectivity of Historical Knowledge', *Philosophy and History*, ed. Raymond Klibansky and H. J. Paton (New York: Harper & Row, 1963), p. 137.

5. Hendrik Kraemer, *Religion and the Christian Faith* (London: Lutterworth Press, 1956), p. 51.

6. *Ibid.*, p. 139.

7. *Ibid.*, p. 143.

8. *Ibid.*, p. 48.

9. *Ibid.*

0. 'On the Character and Married Life of Henry VIII', *Psychoanalysis and History*, ed. Bruce Mazlish (Englewood Cliffs: Prentice-Hall Inc., 1963), p. 126.

1. *Ibid.*, p. 131.

2. *Ibid.*, p. 133.

3. *Ibid.*, p. 138.

4. There may also be interpretive statements which are true but improbable, perhaps because the appropriate evidence is not available to support their probability. The possibility remains that such statements might become probable if further data became available.

5. By descriptive statement I mean the same as factual statement. This differs from Professor Sidney Mead's use of 'fact'. His view, and Carl Becker's, is that when we use the word 'fact' we commonly mean those assertions that are highly probable. The point is that there are statements which are factual or descriptive in intent which are improbable although verifiable in the same way as more certain statements of identical form. We are using the phrase to indicate the intention of the sentence since some statements have another intention. Such a distinction also supports an important difference in the area of fact and interpretation. '...So far as the nature of knowing is concerned there is no fence separating an area of settled "facts" from an area of "interpretation".' ('Church History Explained', *Church History*, 32:1, p. 21). But this is too easy for 'interpretive statements', as we have seen, need verification by at least two methods while factual statements stand on verification by historical method alone.

6. Ernst Benz, 'On Understanding Non-Christian Religions', in Eliade and Kitagawa, *loc. cit.*, p. 121.

7. *Ibid.*

8. Carl Becker, 'What Are Historical Facts?' *The Western Political Quarterly*, VIII, 3, 1955, reprinted in Hans Meyerhoff, *loc. cit.*, p. 122.

9. Louis Gottschalk, 'The Historian's Use of Generalization', *The State of the Social Sciences*, ed. Leonard D. White (Chicago: 1956), p. 437.

0. Becker, *loc. cit.*, p. 131.

1. 'If selection simply means paring down the original list (known to be true), the result of selection will also be true. Any part of a true conjunction remains true.' Morton White, 'Can History Be Objective'? in Hans Meyerhoff, *loc. cit.*, p. 193.

2. Becker, *loc. cit.*, p. 131.

43. Arnold Toynbee, *An Historian's Approach to Religion* (New York: Oxford Universit Press, 1956), p. 9.
44. Hajime Nakamura, *Ways of Thinking of Eastern Peoples* (Honolulu: East-West Cente Press, 1964), p. 47.
45. *Ibid.*, p. 217.
46. *Ibid.*
47. It is true that the very method which involves the strict use of historical evidence implie that one values this method itself. The question, however, is not a valueless historia but whether the historian's values must intrude in the history as written. Such value tend to eliminate bias and values from written history and therefore cannot be appeale to for a refutation of objectivity. That such types of values exist is evidence that all value are not detrimental to objective historical knowledge. The value which proposes t write objective history is certainly a value, but can in itself do nothing but contribute t the goal.
48. An example would be the date of the Exodus or the dates of certain Indian thinkers o documents.
49. Carl Becker, *loc. cit.*
50. Mandelbaum. *loc. cit.*, pp. 203–204.
51. *Ibid.*, p. 204.
52. *Ibid.*, pp. 204–205.
53. John B. Noss, *Man's Religions* (New York: Macmillan, 1963), p. 253.
54. Because historians are unable to rerun experiments and change the variables an constants as the chemist might do, one could hardly speak of 'the' cause of an event i the past. One could, however, speak of 'a' cause with some degree of probability.
55. This is involved in Becker's article and also in Charles Beard, 'Written History as a Act of Faith', Meyerhoff, *loc. cit.*, p. 150.
56. Becker, *loc. cit.*, p. 123.
57. Meyerhoff, *loc. cit.*, p. 199.
58. It is this quite neutral curiosity that Lovejoy contends was his reason for researchin the history of 'the Great Chain of Being', in Arthur Lovejoy, 'Present Standpoints an Past History', Meyerhoff, *loc. cit.*, p. 178.
59. Charles Beard and Sidney Hook, 'Problems in Terminology in Historical Writing' *Theory and Practice in Historical Study* (New York: Social Science Research Counci 1946), p. 246.

NOTES TO 'THE CATEGORY OF UNDERSTANDING'

1. Charles S.J. White, 'A Note on Field Method in Historico-Religious Studies: Th Vallabhasampradāya', *The History of Religions: Essays on the Problem of Under standing*, ed. Joseph M. Kitagawa (Chicago: University of Chicago Press, 1967), p. 16
2. *Ibid.*, p. 163.
3. Joachim Wach, *Das Verstehen, Grundzüge einer Geschichte der hermeneutische Theorie im 19. Jahrhundert*, 3 vols. (Tübingen: Mohr, 1926, 1929, 1933).

4. Kitagawa, *loc. cit.*, p. 7.
5. Joseph M. Kitagawa, 'The History of Religions in America', *The History of Religions: Essays in Methodology*, ed. Joseph M. Kitagawa & Mircea Eliade (Chicago: University of Chicago Press, 1959), p. 28.
6. *Ibid.*, pp. 115ff.
7. Joachim Wach, *The Comparative Study of Religions* (New York: Columbia University Press, 1961), p. 10.
8. *Ibid.*
9. Milton Singer, 'The Rādhā-Krishna *Bhajanas* of Madras City', *Krishna: Myths, Rites, and Attitudes*, ed. Milton Singer (Honolulu: East-West Center Press, 1966), p. 137.
10. Wach, *The Comparative Study of Religions*, p. 10.
11. Frederick J. Streng, *Understanding Religious Man* (Belmont: Dickenson Publishing Company, Inc., 1969), p. 8.
12. *Ibid.*, pp. 6–7.
13. Wach, *The Comparative Study of Religions*, p. 10.
14. Robert F. Spencer, 'The Nature and Value of Functionalism in Anthropology', *Functionalism in the Social Sciences*, ed. Don Martindale (Philadelphia: The American Academy of Political and Social Sciences, 1965), p. 2.
15. I. C. Jarvie, 'Limits to Functionalism and Alternatives to it in Anthropology', *Ibid.*, pp. 18–34.
16. Kingsley Davis, 'The Myth of Functional Analysis as a Special Method in Sociology and Anthropology', *American Sociological Review*, 24:6 (December, 1959), pp. 757–772.
17. Robert K. Merton, *Social Theory and Social Structure*, (New York: The Free Press, 1957), pp. 25ff.
18. Bronislaw Malinowski, A *Scientific Theory of Culture and Other Essays* (New York: Oxford University Press, 1960), pp. 150.
19. Bronislaw Malinowski, 'Anthropology', *The Encyclopaedia Britannica*, Supplementary volumes to Thirteenth Edition, Vol. I, p. 135. *(emphasis Malinowski's)*.
20. *Ibid.*, p. 133.
21. *Ibid.*
22. Merton, *loc. cit.*, p. 32.
23. *Ibid.*, p. 133.
24. Bronislaw Malinowski, *Magic, Science and Religion and Other Essays* (Garden City: Doubleday Anchor, 1954), pp. 30–31.
25. *Ibid.*, pp. 34–35.
26. Malinowski, 'The Role of Magic and Religion', *Reader in Comparative Religion*, ed. William A. Lessa and Evon Z. Vogt (New York: Harper & Row, 1965), p. 106.
27. *Ibid.*, p. 105.
28. *Ibid.*, p. 111.
29. *Ibid.*, p. 112.
30. *Magic, Science and Religion*, p. 39.
31. *Ibid.*, p. 40.

32. *Ibid.*, pp. 40–41.
33. *Ibid.*, p. 49.
34. *Ibid*, pp. 52–53.
35. *Ibid.*, p. 51.
36. *Ibid.*, p. 52.
37. *Ibid.*, p. 45.
38. *Ibid.*
39. *Ibid.*, pp. 46–47.
40. *Ibid.*, p. 97.
41. *Ibid.*, p. 101.
42. *Ibid.*, p. 107.
43. *Ibid.*, p. 146.
44. *Ibid.*, p. 110.
45. *Ibid.*, pp. 112–113.
46. *Ibid.*, p. 62.
47. I. C. Jarvie, *loc. cit.*, p. 22.
48. Robert K. Merton, *loc. cit.*, p. 26.
49. *Ibid.*, p. 32.
50. *Ibid.*, p. 34.
51. Malinowski, *A Scientific Theory of Culture and Other Essays*, p. 170.
52. I. C. Jarvie, *loc. cit.*, p. 28.
53. Robert K. Merton, *loc. cit.*, p. 47.
54. *Ibid.*, pp. 42ff.
55. *Ibid.*, p. 51.
56. *Ibid.*
57. cf. Robert D. Baird, 'Normative Elements in Eliade's Phenomenology of Symbolism' *loc. cit.*
58. Mircae Eliade, *Mephistopheles and the Androgyne* (New York: Sheed and Ward, 1965) pp. 202–203.
59. Mircea Eliade, *Patterns in Comparative Religion*, p. 499. 'Of course this water symbolism is nowhere concretely expressed, it has no central core, for it is made up of a pattern of interdependent symbols which fit together into a system: but it is nonetheless real for that.'
60. *Ibid.*
61. *Ibid.*, p. 450.
62. Mirecea Eliade, *Images and Symbols* (New York: Sheed and Ward, 1961), pp. 24ff
63. *Patterns in Comparative Religion*, p. 450. 'The primitive mind did genuinely have the experience of seeing each hierophany in the framework of the symbolism it implied and did always really *see* that symbolic system in every fragment which went to make it up.' (*emphasis Eliade's*).
64. *Ibid.*
65. *Images and Symbols*, p. 37.
66. *Ibid.*, p. 25. 'Symbols and myths come from such depths: they are part and parcel of the

human being, and it is impossible that they should not be found again in any and every existential situation of man in the Cosmos.'

67. Mircea Eliade, *The Sacred and the Profane: The Nature of Religion*, trans. Willard R. Trask (New York: Harper & Brothers, 1961), p. 95.

68. Mircea Eliade, *Myth and Reality*, trans. Willard R. Trask (New York: Harper & Row, Publishers, 1963), pp. 8ff.

69 *The Sacred and the Profane*, p. 97.

70. *Myth and Reality*, p. 22.

71. *Ibid.*, p. 18.

72. *The Sacred and the Profane*, p. 98.

73. *Ibid.*, p. 99.

74. *Ibid.*, p. 100. *(emphasis Eliade's)*.

75. *Patterns in Comparative Religion*, p. 413.

76. *Ibid.*, p. 415.

77. *Ibid.*, p. 414.

78. *Ibid.*, pp. 415–416.

79. *Myth and Reality*, p. 141.

80. *Ibid.*, p. 140.

81. *Ibid.*, pp. 184–185.

82. Mircea Eliade, *Rites and Symbols of Initiation: The Mysteries of Birth and Rebirth*, Trans. Willard R. Trask (New York: Harper & Row, 1965), p. x.

83. *Ibid.*, p. xv.

84. *Ibid.*

85. *Ibid.*, p. 1.

86. *Ibid.*, p. 3. *(emphasis Eliade's)*.

87. *Ibid.*, p. 6.

88. *Ibid.*, p. 7.

89. *Ibid.*

90. *Ibid.*, p. 9.

91. *Ibid.*, p. 8.

92. *Ibid.*, p. 9.

93. *Ibid.*, p. 4.

94. *Ibid.*, p. 15.

95. *Ibid.*

96. *Ibid.*, p. 16.

97. *Ibid.*

98. *Ibid.*, p. 128

99. C.J. Bleeker, *The Sacred Bridge*, p. 23.

100. *Mephistopheles and the Androgyne*, p. 195.

101. *Ibid.*

102. Cf. C. J. Bleeker, 'The Phenomenological Method', *The Sacred Bridge*, p. 7. 'In my opinion the phenomenology of religion is an empirical science without philosophical aspirations.'

103. 'Methodological Remarks on the Study of Religious Symbolism', ed. Mircea Eliade and Joseph M. Kitagawa, *The History of Religions: Essays in Methodology*, p. 92. *(emphasis Eliade's)*.
104. Mircea Eliade, 'Crisis and Renewal in the History of Religions', *History of Religions* 5 (1965), pp. 1–17.
105. *Ibid.*, p. 7. 'But in the case of the History of Religions, hermeneutics shows itself to be a more complex operation for it is not only a question of comprehending and inter-preting the "religious facts". Because of their nature these religious facts constitute a material on which one can think – or even ought to think – and think in a creative manner, just as did Montesquieu, Voltaire, Herder, Hegel when they applied them-selves to the task of thinking about human institutions and their history.'
106. *Ibid.*, p. 8.
107. Eliade urges that if general theories are not produced by historians of religions who are most familiar with the religious facts, then 'we shall continue to submit to the audacious and irrelevant interpretations of religious realities made by psychologists, sociologists or devotees of various reductionist ideologies'. In 'Crisis and Renewal in the History of Religions', *loc. cit.*, p. 16. If historians of religions do not complete their theoretical work the 'autonomous discipline' may die. 'In this case we must expect a slow but irrevocable process of decomposition, which will end in the disappearance of the History of Religions as an autonomous discipline.', *Ibid.*
108. Willard Gurdon Oxtoby, 'Religionswissenschaft Revisited', *Religions in Antiquity*, ed Jacob Neusner (Leiden: E. J. Brill, 1968), p. 597.
109. Cf. p. 108.
110. Heinz Robert Schlette, *Towards a Theology of Religions* (New York: Herder and Herder, 1966), p. 53.
111. Wilfred Cantwell Smith, 'The Comparative Study of Religion', *Inaugural Lectures* (Montreal: McGill University, 1950), p. 42.
112. Kitagawa and Eliade (editors), *The History of Religions: Essays in Methodology* p. 34.
113. *Ibid.*
114. *Ibid.*, p. 42.
115. Wilfred Cantwell Smith, *The Meaning and End of Religion: A New Approach to the Religious Traditions of Mankind* (New York: The Macmillan Company, 1963), p. 12
116. *Ibid.*, p. 17.
117. Wilfred Cantwell Smith, *The Faith of Other Men* (New York: New American Library 1963).
118. *The Meaning and End of Religion*, p. 12.
119. *Ibid.*, p. 29.
120. *Ibid.*
121. *Ibid.*, p. 19.
122. *Ibid.*, p. 39.
123. *Ibid.*, p. 43
124. *Ibid.*, p. 47.

125. *Ibid.*, pp. 65–66.
126. *Ibid.*, p. 69.
127. We have indicated in chapter two the grounds on which such a question could be answered.
128. *The Meaning and End of Religion*, p. 71
129. *Ibid.*, p. 114.
130. *Ibid.*, p. 118.
131. *Ibid.*, p. 127.
132. *Ibid.*, p. 141.
133. *Ibid.*, p. 142.
134. *Ibid.*, p. 144.
135. *Ibid.*, p. 145.
136. *Ibid.*, p. 156.
137. *Ibid.*
138. *Ibid.*, pp. 156–157.
139. *Ibid.*, p. 185.
140. *Ibid.*, p. 188.
141. *The Faith of Other Men*, pp. 39–52.
142. *Ibid.*, p. 44.
143. *Ibid.*, pp. 44–45.
144. *Ibid.*, p. 45.
145. *Ibid.*, p. 50.
146. *Ibid.*
147. *Ibid.*, p. 51.
148. *Ibid.*, p. 52.
149. *Ibid.*
150. Wilfred Cantwell Smith, *Questions of Religious Truth* (New York: Charles Scribner's Sons, 1967.)
151. *Ibid.*, p. 74.
152. *Ibid.*, p. 76.
153. *Ibid.*, pp. 75–76.
154. *Ibid.*, p. 67.
155. *Ibid.*, p. 71.
156. *Ibid.*, p. 79.
157. *Ibid.*, p. 68.
158. *Ibid.*, p. 72.
159. *Ibid.*, p. 82.
160. Cf. Smith's admission of this point in *The Faith of Other Men*, p. 43.
161. *Ibid.*, p. 46. *(emphasis mine)*.
162. Hendrik Kraemer, *Religion and the Christian Faith* (London: Lutterworth Press, 1956), p. 45.
163. *Ibid.*, p. 48.
164. *Ibid.*, p. 52.

165. *Ibid.*, p. 144.
166. *Ibid.*, p. 166.
167. *Ibid.*, p. 144.
168. *Ibid.*, p. 145.
169. *Ibid.*, p. 146.
170. *Ibid.*, p. 46.
171. p. 252. *(emphasis Kraemer's)*
172. *Ibid.*, p. 82.
173. *Ibid.*, p. 356.
174. *Ibid.*, p. 357.
175. *Ibid.*, p. 350.
176. *Ibid.*, p. 351.
177. *Ibid.*, p. 354.
178. *Ibid.*, p. 323.
179. *Ibid.*, p. 324.
180. *Ibid.*, p. 326.
181. *Ibid.*, p. 331.
182. *Ibid.*, p. 334.
183. *Ibid.*, p. 337.
184. *Ibid.*
185. *Ibid.*, p. 18.
186. Quoted in Hans Küng, 'The World Religions in God's Plan of Salvation', *Christian Revelation and World Religions*, ed. J. Neuner, S. J. (London: Burnes & Oates, 1967), p. 34.
187. *Ibid.*, p. 38.
188. *Ibid.*, p. 41.
189. *Ibid.*, p. 42.
190. *Ibid.*, p. 46.
191. *Ibid.*
192. *Ibid.*, p. 52.
193. *Ibid.*, p. 53.
194. *Ibid.*, p. 52.
195. *Ibid.*, pp. 53–54.
196. *Ibid.*, p. 55.
197. *Ibid.*
198. *Ibid.*, p. 59.
199. *Ibid.*, pp. 47–48.
200. *Ibid.*, pp. 48–49.
201. Contained in S. Radhakrishnan, *East and West in Religion* (London: George Allen & Unwin, 1933).
202. *Ibid.*, p. 22.
203. *Ibid.*, p. 16.
204. *Ibid.*, p. 18.

205. *Ibid.*, p. 26.
206. *Ibid.*, p. 19.
207. Quoted in *East and West in Religion*, pp. 27–28.
208. *Ibid.*, p. 37.
209. *Ibid.*, p. 38.
210. *Ibid.*
211. Cf. Donald Walhout, *Interpreting Religion* (Englewood Cliffs: Prentice Hall, 1963), pp. 437ff.

NOTES TO 'SOME INADEQUATE CATEGORIES'

1. His argument is more fully developed in *The Meaning and End of Religion*.
2. *Ibid.*, p. 50.
3. *Ibid.*, p. 19.
4. Paul Tillich, *Systematic Theology* (Chicago: University of Chicago Press, 1963), III, p. 130.
5. Smith, *loc. cit.*, p. 191.
6. *Ibid.*, p. 128.
7. *Ibid.*, p. 129.
8. Cf. *Eastern Religions and Western Thought; Religion and Society; East and West in Religion.* In this same context one might ask what meaning might any longer be given to J. Sinha, *The Foundation of Hinduism* or T. M. P. Mahadevan, *Outlines of Hinduism.* Both of the authors are 'Hindus'.
9. Smith himself rejects the 'nature and origin' theory, whereby one limits a religion to its original form and sees subsequent developments as aberrations. The faithful application of his principle makes the question of who originated the term quite irrelevant to the religious question. Cf. *The Meaning and End of Religion*, p. 148.
10. 'The Key Word of Religion', *The Sacred Bridge*, p. 36.
11. *Ibid.*, p. 42.
12. We have rejected the use of 'essence' in chapter one on analytic grounds. Here we show the circularity involved in the *historical* search for essences.
13. 'The "Entelecheia" of Religious Phenomena', *The Sacred Bridge*, p. 21.
14. Tillich, as a theologian, also makes a normative distinction between valid and invalid ultimate concerns. While this is certainly a legitimate question, it is not necessary on the historical level. Ultimate concern, used as a functional definition, contains no norm for distinguishing valid from invalid ultimate concerns. What it offers is a criterion for *identifying* religion, not for *evaluating* it. It provides the possibility of beginning our historical work by indicating *what* we are studying when we say we are studying religion, but it does not have built into it a decision as to what is the *true* religion if there is one. Our argument that defining religion in terms of ultimate concern is non-judgmental is based on *the way the definition is being used*, namely as a means of identifying the religious, not as a means of determining ontological truth.

15. *An Historian's Approach to Religion* (New York: Oxford University Press, 1956), Chapter 19.
16. *Ibid.*, p. 266.
17. For the list of 'essential counsels and truths' see *Ibid.*, pp. 274–275.
18. See my later discussions on 'syncretism'.
19. I will refer to these and other such categories as 'the religions'.
20. *The Meaning and End of Religion*, p. 132.
21. *Ibid.*, p. 135.
22. *Ibid.*, p. 142.
23. I will return to this point when discussing the search for the essence of 'the religions'.
24. *The Bhagavad Gītā*, trans. Franklin Edgerton (New York: Harper and Row, 1964), 72, 154.
25. 'Comparative Religion: Whither – and Why?' in *The History of Religions: Essays in Methodology*, p. 52.
26. Such radical religious change can be documented in *any* of 'the religions'.
27. There is also the possibility of what might be termed the temperary elevation of the penultimate. Both Gandhi and Aurobindo Ghose held that liberation was man's ideal goal. However, historical circumstances forced them to concentrate on the admittedly penultimate concern (for them) of national independence. It is their testimony, however, that they never lose sight of what is the ultimate goal of man. Whether one is considering the temporary elevation of the penultimate in such cases or rather a form of imminent or mundane religion can only be determined by a close examination of the available data.
28. Joseph Kitagawa, *Religion in Japanese History* (New York: Columbia University Press, 1966). This is not necessarily a conscious concern on the part of Kitagawa to eliminate such categories which do occur in the body of his text.
29. Edward Conze, *Buddhism: Its Essence and Development* (New York: Harper and Row, 1959).
30. Kenneth Morgan (ed.), *The Path of the Buddha* (New York: Ronald Press, 1956).
31. Richard Robinson, *Early Madhymika in India and China* (Madison: University of Wisconsin Press, 1967).
32. Nihar-Ranjan Ray, *An Introduction to the Study of Theravada Buddhism in Burma* (Calcutta: University of Calcutta, 1946).
33. See our later discussion of syncretism.
34. Melford E. Spiro, *Burmese Supernaturalism* (Englewood Cliffs, New Jersey: Prentice-Hall, Inc., 1967), p. 279.
35. '...Because there are so many varieties within Buddhism as to make the single term "Buddhist" too general for accurate use, it is Southern Buddhism that is here compared with Christianity.' *Buddhism and Christianity* (Philadelphia: Westminster Press, 1963), pp. 10–11.
36. *Ibid.*, p. 152.
37. *Ibid.*, p. 155.
38. *Ibid.*, pp. 154–155.
39. It should be observed that we do not suggest 'Indian Religions', 'Chinese Religions',

'Japanese Religions', etc., which would be as inadequate as 'the religions'. The areas are simply designated as convenient ways of dividing the effort of religious study. They are not to be taken as new *secondary categories*. To attempt to ascertain an 'Indian Mind' or an 'Indian Mentality' would be as misdirected as the search for the essence of 'Hinduism'.

40. *The Christian Message in a Non-Christian World* (Grand Rapids: Kregel Publications, 1963), pp. 200–211. First published in 1938. *Religion and the Christian Faith* (London: Lutterworth Press, 1956), pp. 387–417. Asked to contribute an article to *The Theology of the Christian Mission*, Kraemer responded with a letter indicating that he could say little on the subject that he had not already said.
41. *Religion and the Christian Faith*, p. 389.
42. *Ibid.*, p. 406.
43. *Ibid.*, p. 297 *(emphasis mine)*.
44. *Ibid.*, pp. 200 and 401.
45. *Ibid.*, p. 389.
46. S. Radhakrishnan, *East and West in Religion* (London: George Allen & Unwin, Ltd. 1933), p. 62.
47. Kraemer, *loc. cit.*, pp. 390–391.
48 'Syncretism' in *The Oxford Dictionary of the Christian Church* (London: Oxford University Press, 1957), p. 1314.
49. Kraemer, *loc. cit.*, p. 392.
50. William Ernest Hocking, *The Coming World Civilization* (New York: Harper & Brothers, Publishers, 1956), p. 146.
51. H. R. Mackintosh, *Types of Modern Theology* (London: Nisbet and Co., Ltd., 1956), p. 185.
52. Hocking, *loc. cit.*, p. 147.
53. Cf. John B. Noss, *Man's Religions* (New York: The Macmillan Company, 1963) third edition, p. 436. Also D. C. Holtom, *The National Faith of Japan* (London: Kegan Paul, Trench, Trubner & Company Ltd., 1938), p. 38.
54. Kraemer, *loc. cit.*, p. 401.
55. S. Das Gupta, *A. History of Indian Philosophy* (Cambridge: Cambridge University Press, 1922), Vol. I, p. 446.
56. Kraemer, *loc. cit.*, p. 201.
57. *Ibid.* Cf. also Noss and Holtom.
58. Holtom, *loc. cit.*, p. 38.
59. Smith, *The Meaning and End of Religion*, p. 2.
60. M. Anesaki, *History of Japanese Religion* (London: Kegan Paul, Trench, Trubner & Company Ltd., 1930), p. 137.
61. Kraemer, *loc. cit.*, p. 402.
62. *Ibid.*, p. 403.
63. *The Christian Message in a Non-Christian World*, p. 203.
64. William Montgomery Watt, *Truth in the Religions* (Edinburgh: Edinburgh University Press, 1963), p. 61.

Index